AMBASSADORS
of
RECONCILIATION

Volume II

AMBASSADORS

of

RECONCILIATION

VOLUME II

DIVERSE CHRISTIAN PRACTICES OF
RESTORATIVE JUSTICE AND PEACEMAKING

ELAINE ENNS & CHED MYERS

ORBIS BOOKS

Maryknoll, New York 10545

Founded in 1970, Orbis Books endeavors to publish works that enlighten the mind, nourish the spirit, and challenge the conscience. The publishing arm of the Maryknoll Fathers and Brothers, Orbis seeks to explore the global dimensions of the Christian faith and mission, to invite dialogue with diverse cultures and religious traditions, and to serve the cause of reconciliation and peace. The books published reflect the views of their authors and do not represent the official position of the Maryknoll Society. To learn more about Maryknoll and Orbis Books, please visit our website at www.maryknollsociety.org.

Published by Orbis Books, Maryknoll, NY 10545-0302.

Manufactured in the United States of America.

Library of Congress Cataloguing-in-Publication Data

Myers, Ched.
    Ambassadors of reconciliation / Ched Myers and Elaine Enns.
      p. cm.
    Includes bibliographical references.
    ISBN 978-1-57075-833-1 (pbk. : v. 2)
    1. Restorative justice—Biblical teaching. 2. Bible. N.T.—Criticism, interpretation, etc.
I. Enns, Elaine. II. Title.
    BS2545.J8M94   2009
    261.8—dc22
                            2008049652

*To Margaret and Beno Enns
and Mary and Gordon Cosby*

While Love Is Unfashionable

While love is unfashionable
let us live
unfashionably.
Seeing the world
a complex ball
in small hands;
love our blackest garment.
Let us be poor
in all but truth, and courage
handed down
by the old
spirits.
Let us be intimate with
ancestral ghosts
and music
of the undead.

While love is dangerous
let us walk bareheaded
beside the Great River.
Let us gather blossoms
under fire.

—Alice Walker (1991: 233)

CONTENTS

FOREWORD

If you want to read about conflict resolution, you have an abundance of choices. Similarly, there is a large and rapidly growing literature on restorative justice, on nonviolent activism, and on peacemaking in general. Numerous books analyze violence and its roots as well as the dynamics of power and privilege. Few, however, attempt to bring all these together in a practical, integrated framework.[1]

Unfortunately, the fragmented nature of this published literature reflects the reality on the ground. People who work in conflict resolution, for example, rarely realize the potential restorative justice offers for addressing the justice dynamics inherent in conflict. Likewise, peacemakers may write off justice advocates as troublemakers, while nonviolent activists often see peacemakers as glossing over underlying wrongs. Those of us in these fields don't interact with one another enough, nor do we often see ourselves as working toward the same goals.

To bring these approaches together, Enns and Myers offer the metaphor of "full-spectrum" peacemaking. Each of the quadrants in this spectrum has an important part to play in creating what my colleague John Paul Lederach has called "justpeace," or what the biblical tradition calls *shalom*: right relationships with one another, the creation, and our Creator. To truly work in this direction, however, each of us must recognize our connections and contributions to the whole.

Enns and Myers don't just bring us together; they also challenge us to go deeper. Building true justice and peace requires that we do more than work at immediate, "presenting" injustices and conflicts. We must also be aware of and address underlying factors that contribute to and shape conflict, such as inequities of power and privilege and structural injustice. Fortunately, the authors offer analytic tools to help understand these dynamics.

Their full-spectrum peacemaking provides an intuitive and practical framework for understanding how the work fits together and the place that each approach has within it. The authors use the metaphor of a tree, acknowledging the importance of attention not only to the roots of our life

---

1. An exception is Lisa Schirch, *The Little Book of Strategic Peacebuilding* (Intercourse, PA: Good Books, 2004).

together, but also to the soil that nourishes it and the way that the various branches of peacemaking can contribute to a just and peaceful world.

Enns and Myers bring to their marriage (yes, they are a couple) and to this book practical backgrounds of experience in restorative justice, conflict resolution, and nonviolent activism. They speak from these real-world places, but they also acknowledge their limits and blind spots as relatively privileged European North Americans. So they have also listened to, learned from, and here offer to us voices of those who have directly experienced the harms of violence and oppression and those who are actively working to address these harms. That is the focus of the second part of this book.

The authors have an ambitious goal in this two-volume series: to bring an integrated Christian perspective to the work of justice and peacebuilding for both practitioners and interested laypeople. As an academic and practitioner who is committed to connecting with the same audiences, I believe they have succeeded. While their perspective is Christian, it is not exclusively so, and much in this volume will be of interest to non-Christians. And although (hallelujah!) the volume is not written in formal academic language, those of us in the academic world will learn from it as well.

Howard Zehr
Professor of Restorative Justice
Center for Justice & Peacebuilding
Eastern Mennonite University
Harrisonburg, VA

ACKNOWLEDGMENTS

This project arose from a conversation between us that began the weekend we met and has continued on since (see below, 2A). We are grateful for the many ways we have each been drawn by the other into new experiences and understandings as a result.

Our thinking has been enriched by a decade of dialogue, formal and informal, with many colleagues. The material in these volumes has been shared in various stages and forms across a broad ecumenical and geographic spectrum, from the seminary to the sanctuary to the streets.[1] We are indebted to Duke Chapel in Durham for a two-month writing fellowship that gave us respite from a demanding travel schedule in order to wrestle the manuscript into shape. Conversations with various staff members of Mennonite Central Committee United States and Canada have been important, as has the encouragement of Howard Zehr (rightly considered the father of the contemporary restorative justice movement) and colleagues at the Center for Peacemaking and Conflict Studies at Fresno Pacific University. We thank these friends for their interest and critical feedback, and hope this project makes a useful contribution to the

---

1. Venues included: American Baptist Seminary of the West (Berkeley); Luther Theological Seminary (Saskatoon); Fresno Pacific University, CA; Andover Newton Theological Seminary (Boston); Menno Simons College and University of Winnipeg, MB; Claremont School of Theology, CA; Christian Brothers University and Rhodes College (Memphis); Memphis Theological Seminary; Manchester College (IN); the ELM Center (Sydney) and the Commission for Mission (Melbourne) of the Uniting Church in Australia; the National Restorative Justice Conference (San Antonio); Montreat (NC) and Ghost Ranch (NM) Presbyterian Retreat Centers; St. Benedict's Retreat Center (Winnipeg); Five Oaks Center (ON) and Calling Lakes Center (SK) of the United Church of Canada; East Belfast Mission (Northern Ireland); London Mennonite Center; Word and World Schools; the Franciscan Sisters of Clinton, IA; the Mennonite Peace and Justice Network; the Anglican Social Justice desk of New Zealand/Aotearoa; the Methodist Federation of Social Action; the Center for Restorative Justice Works of the Archdiocese of Los Angeles; Christians Empowered for Reconciliation and Justice (Los Angeles); Christian Peacemaker Teams Congress; Sojourners; the Beloved Community Center (Greensboro); United Methodist Pastors Assembly, New England; the Resource Center for Nonviolence (Santa Cruz); Youth Justice Facility team, Northern Cheyenne Reservation (MT); First Presbyterian Church of Palo Alto, CA; Winchester United Church of Christ (MA); the Sacramento Mediation Center; Baptist Peace Fellowship of North America; and the Ecumenical Institute of the Northeast.

ongoing development of restorative justice and peacemaking thought and practice.

The support of the board and staff of Bartimaeus Cooperative Ministries has been key to the completion of this project; they encouraged us at every step on what turned out to be a longer-than-anticipated path of writing. Peg Rosenkrands provided seed money for volume II; indeed, all of our BCM donors have made this work possible. Sara Hansen Sera gifted Elaine with immensely helpful coaching in writing up the interviews. Robert Ellsberg suggested that this project appear in two volumes, and we appreciate our partnership with Orbis Books. Readers interested in corresponding with us about this project can reach us through our website: www.bcm-net.org (inquiries@bcm-net.org).

It is the witness of our interviewees that gives credence to this project, and each was patient and gracious from the beginning to the end of our process, which took in some cases almost three years. These individuals are formidable disciples, and we are grateful to call them friends. We pray that we have been faithful storytellers.

Elaine dedicates these volumes to her parents, Margaret and Beno Enns, in gratitude for having been raised faithfully in the peaceable spirit of the Mennonite tradition. Ched dedicates them to Gordon and Mary Cosby of the Church of the Savior in Washington, DC, for their understanding of and solidarity with his vocation over the last ten years. Our deepest respect goes to these elders in the faith for their sustaining love.

May the church make known the manifold wisdom of God to the principalities and powers (Eph 3:10).

INTRODUCTION

This is the second of two volumes exploring a theology and practice of faith-rooted restorative justice and peacemaking. Volume I looks at four key New Testament texts that together represent a theological foundation for this work. Our interpretations there are conducted in conversation with the life and witness of Martin Luther King, Jr., our greatest North American apostle of nonviolence. Volume II, in turn, analyzes the contemporary terrain of restorative justice and peacemaking in North America (part 1), and profiles the exemplary work of nine practitioners who are incarnating the scriptural vision in real life contexts of profound violence and injustice (part 2).

We reiterate here our working definition of restorative justice and peacemaking as: "a range of nonviolent responses to injustice, violation, and/or violence with the aim of

1. reducing or halting the presenting violence in order that
2. victims and offenders (as well as their communities and other stakeholders) can collectively identify harms, needs, and responsibilities so that
3. they can determine how to make things as right as possible, which can include covenants of accountability, restitution, reparations and (ideally) reconciliation."

We are keenly aware of the debate in the field over which broad rubric, if any, best captures this kind of work. Transformative justice, conflict management, peace-building, and violence-reduction have all been proposed, and each has its merits. We have chosen to use "restorative justice and peacemaking" for two reasons. One is to insist that these two trajectories, though often seen as divergent, should in fact converge and are ultimately inseparable. The other is to broaden and deepen the understandings and practices associated with each term.[1] We are not, however, interested in debates about parlance, and hope our collegial readers who prefer other rubrics will focus on the substance rather than the semantics of this study.

---

1. We explore these issues further below in chapter 2 and add cautions about some problems in contemporary practices in chapter 3.

The challenge facing those of us who promote alternatives to retribution and violence is to understand and learn from one another's methods and to resist becoming proprietary about "branding."

Part 1 begins by articulating a concern that our North American restorative justice and peacemaking movements aren't always sufficiently broad or deep in our diagnoses of, and thus our responses to, the epidemic of violence that plagues our world. We revisit the "spiral of violence" model developed by Brazilian Archbishop Dom Helder Camara in the late 1960s to guide us in our diagnostic work (chapter 1). We next note the lack of communication and collaboration between various branches of the historic tree of peacemaking. As an example we offer our own experience of the gulf between our respective worlds of restorative justice facilitation and mediation (Elaine) and nonviolent activism (Ched). We then propose an integral model of "full-spectrum peacemaking" (chapter 2). Finally we tackle the persistent question of how realities of privilege influence (and undermine) restorative justice and peacemaking work in the First World. As practitioners and teachers who are white and middle class, we are committed to giving particular attention to issues of race, gender, and class difference, and to being diligent about mapping social power (chapter 3).

Part 2 introduces colleagues whose work we think represents pioneering responses to violence and injustice. We interviewed:

- two restorative justice practitioners who have faced worst case scenario crimes involving loss of life (chapter 4);
- two peacemakers who have made deeply personal responses to the public violence of war (chapter 5);
- two women who have stood fiercely against systems of dehumanizing violence (chapter 6); and
- two men who have taken up the challenge of healing historic injustice (chapter 7).

We used three criteria for selecting these testimonies. Each interviewee

1. *is someone we know personally and/or whose work we are familiar with and respect highly.* Though a few of these stories have received some media exposure, none of our subjects can be considered "famous." It is our hope that the example of ordinary disciples doing extraordinary work would be as motivating, but not as intimidating, as one more "hagiography" of Harriet Tubman or Mohandas Gandhi or Cesar Chavez.
2. *is involved in cutting-edge work that in our opinion pushes the boundaries of engaged restorative justice and peacemaking.* The practices

profiled here are in several cases not typical of what is usually discussed in the contemporary literature. What better way to promote and challenge the field than by learning from those working
at its frontiers?
3. *works from Christian convictions.* There are, of course, many who
engage in this work from different spiritual orientations, as well as
many who do not embrace religious understandings at all. As noted
in volume I, however, our project focuses on the formidable task of
motivating and resourcing the Christian churches to reclaim *their*
vocational identity as peacemakers. Moreover, we are cognizant of
the long history of violation and violence in which Christendom
has been complicit. In the spirit of Jesus' admonition to "make peace
with your accuser . . ." before proceeding with worship (Matt 5:23-
26), our churches ought to make restorative justice and peacemaking their most urgent priority.

We decided for reasons of length and audience to limit our profiles to persons
who, like ourselves, have been socially formed in the North American context (Elaine is from Saskatchewan, Ched is Californian). We therefore did
not include in this project any of the inspiring work that originates elsewhere
around the world. This was a difficult delimitation, given remarkable international stories of faith-rooted restorative justice and peacemaking such as:

- the courageous nonviolence of Las Abejas in Chiapas;[2]
- the groundbreaking restorative justice work occurring in New
  Zealand/Aotearoa;[3]
- the conciliatory work of JustaPaz in Colombia;[4]
- the witness of the ecumenical Corrymeela community in Northern Ireland;[5]
- or truth and reconciliation work in many violence-scarred countries around the world.[6]

However, because the United States continues to be, as Dr. King put it
in his famous Riverside Speech, "the greatest purveyor of violence in the

---

2. See Tavanti (2002) and Kovic (2003), as well as the following websites: www
.cgtchiapas.org; www.derechoshumanos.org.mx/modules.php?name=News&file=article&sid
=383; and http://piwdw.org/news/mexico/chiapan_pacifist_group_is_firs/.

3. See Consedine (1999); Consedine and Bowen (1999); www.restorativejustice.org.nz/;
and www.justice.govt.nz/restorative-justice/. A good database for restorative justice work
around the world is www.restorativejustice.org.

4. See www.justapaz.org.

5. See www.corrymeela.org; Cichon (2000).

6. See e.g. Avruch and Vejarano (2002).

world," we concluded that there is ample justification for focusing on our own house.[7]

We acknowledge other limitations. We do not, for example, look at the influential work of Alternatives to Violence Projects in prisons, or the international peace-building work of John Paul Lederach, or other well-known efforts, because of the literature already available.[8] Though Harley Eagle (below, 3B) and Lawrence Hart (below, 7A) are part of the vibrant movement among indigenous people to rehabilitate their traditions of restorative justice, we do not discuss native sentencing circles and other alternatives to western criminal justice.[9] We would have liked to include stories of restorative justice and peacemaking work on issues such as full inclusion for sexual minorities; immigrant rights; sexual abuse in the churches; and the environmental crisis. Again, however, we were constrained by the length of this project.[10] And we are mindful of the problems that come with a focus on individuals rather than on movements or organizations (summarized below in the Introduction to part 2). We are consoled by the fact that no one book can capture all the ways that practitioners are embodying restorative justice and peacemaking in our violence-ridden world today.

We approach this field, with its fluid and rapid state of development, as if working a jigsaw puzzle: looking from different angles to discern major characteristics, to find edges, and to see what's missing. To reiterate our double goal for this project:

1. For those unfamiliar with faith-rooted restorative justice and peacemaking, we seek to provide a primer that summarizes key concepts and practices, and to point to further resources. We believe these ways of thinking and doing can transform both the church's internal life and its public witness.

---

7. See Washington (1986:231ff.); we comment on this speech in volume I, chapter 2.

8. On Alternatives to Violence work see www.avpusa.org. Walter Wright has posted a Lederach bibliography at www.mediate.com/articles/wrightW2.cfm; see also Lederach and Jenner (2002).

9. For resources on indigenous traditions of restorative justice, see Ross (1996); Rudin (2005); Dickson-Gilmore and La Prairie (2005); and Mirsky (n.d.). See also below, chapter 3, n. 4.

10. A notable example of faith-oriented nonviolent activism for lesbian, gay, bisexual, and transgendered rights is Soulforce (www.soulforce.org). One of the finest church-oriented groups involved in immigrant rights is Borderlinks (www.borderlinks.org). On sexual abuse in the churches, see Fortune and Marshall (2004). An excellent example of environmental justice is the nonviolent campaign to stop illegal logging on indigenous land at the Asubpee-schoseewagong First Nation (Grassy Narrows, Ontario), supported by Christian Peacemaker Teams; see http://friendsofgrassynarrows.com/ and www.turtleisland.org/discussion/view-topic.php?t=445; www.cpt.org/canada/kenora.php.

2. For experienced faith-rooted practitioners, we hope to advance a vigorous conversation about how to broaden and deepen our theological and analytical understandings and concrete engagements.

While this volume cannot possibly cover every aspect of restorative justice and peacemaking, nor offer great detail on any one aspect, we do trust it offers an overview that is both representative and evocative.

May the analytical and narrative explorations herein inspire, embolden, and encourage a new generation of ambassadors of reconciliation.

Part One

Models for Integral Restorative Justice and Peacemaking in North America

In order to contextualize the concerns of this book, we begin with three chapters that offer models to help us think about our work. Chapter 1 offers a diagnostic model, mapping the relationship between behavioral and social violence. Looking at the roots of the problem is crucial to any practice of healing and transformation; otherwise we are forever addressing symptoms. Chapter 2 examines the fracturing of North American restorative justice and peacemaking movements over the last quarter century, particularly the divergence between "mediation" and "direct action" styles of violence reduction. We then propose a second model that affirms an inclusive and integral "toolbox" for nonviolent intervention in the spiral of violence. Chapter 3 reflects on the crucial question of social power, analyzing how it can and should be mapped as part of restorative justice and peacemaking work. Colleague Harley Eagle then offers thoughts about why those who are privileged by race, gender, and class must pay careful attention to these issues.

All three chapters build on existing models already in use among some of our colleagues. We have refined and expanded these conceptual frameworks in presentations to gatherings of restorative justice and peace colleagues over the last several years. They are works in progress and should be further revised as experience instructs us. If readers fear getting bogged down in these somewhat theoretical discussions, they are free to engage part 2 first, and return to this section afterward.

1

PROBING THE ROOTS OF VIOLENCE

The ultimate weakness of violence is that it is a descending spiral, begetting the very thing it seeks to destroy. . . . In fact, violence merely increases hate. . . . Returning violence for violence multiplies violence, adding deeper darkness to a night already devoid of stars.
—Martin Luther King, Jr. (1967: 62)

One Sunday morning during the year we were writing this book, we heard shouting out on the street. We ran outside to find two groups of young men squaring off at the corner, and realized immediately that our simmering neighborhood "troubles" had sparked up again. A group of white teenagers were taunting the Mexican family across the street from us, and it was about to come to blows. With two other neighbors we moved straight into the fray, and, positioning ourselves between the two groups, we managed to back the white kids slowly down the street.

For the next hour we shuttled back and forth between the two groups, now a block apart, listening to accusations and cursing while attempting to calm them down. Twenty minutes after we had defused the confrontation, three sheriff's cars showed up (at which point the white kids hastily threw their knives behind some bushes). The officers soon left—after all, they told us, there had been no actual bloodshed.

Our small blue collar town, about sixty miles north of Los Angeles, is not immune to larger social conflicts. Historically, minority Latino residents have been victims of repeated racial harassment and discrimination. Angry and wanting to fight back, some young Latinos have formed gangs that periodically skirmish with white kids, some of whom dress as "skinheads" and profess white supremacy.

That morning the white teenagers were complaining about how "those Mexicans" are always whistling, throwing gang signs, and jumping their friends. They claimed they were just protecting themselves, but belied their true sentiments by peppering their account with racist slurs. Our

3

Mexican neighbors, on the other hand, claimed that the "skinheads" are always cruising by, throwing stones at the house and harassing them, trying to start a rumble.

Before everyone dispersed that morning, we told each group of young men three things:

- This was our neighborhood too, and we would not tolerate fighting and racial taunting. We didn't want to see anyone get hurt *or* go to jail.
- We would be out in the street whenever trouble was brewing, so they would have to go through us to get at one another—and we assumed they really didn't want to be beating on some nice older white folks.
- We hoped we could eventually get both groups to sit down and listen to one another, to try to move beyond this long-standing rivalry.

There have been subsequent attacks, and we haven't been able to get the kids to talk with one another. But the neighborhood is more organized as a result of several community meetings.

We have, however, learned more about the young men in each group. Because of patterns of family disruption and dysfunction, most live with their grandmothers. Several from each side have dropped out of school and/or done time in juvenile hall or jail, though all deny being gang members. They complain of a lack of jobs and opportunity, and for the Mexicans, a long-standing pattern of racist treatment by the police and at school. We learned that the two toughest white kids endured horrible conditions at home.

This local conflict struck us as a parable about the problems and prospects of trying to practice restorative justice and peacemaking in the real world. There was nothing extraordinary, much less heroic, about our response to that Sunday episode. The four of us who intervened are veterans of justice advocacy and violence-reduction work, from victim-offender facilitation to breaking up street fights in inner city Los Angeles to refugee accompaniment in Salvadoran war zones. But our little corner skirmish confirmed to us the central theses we explore in part 1: (1) all behavioral violence has social roots; (2) the work of restorative justice and peacemaking is necessarily variegated, yet of a whole cloth; and (3) understanding how social power is distributed is key to responding to conflict.

Addressing our neighborhood problem will require at least three sets of peacemaking "tools" (see below, 2B):

- To disrupt incipient violence draws on skills of nonviolent direct action;

- To hold a tentative truce, while familiarizing ourselves with each side of the conflict, draws on the skills of arbitration and peace-keeping; and
- To bring the hostile parties together to work out their differences without fighting draws on the art of mediation of facilitated dialogue.

But ultimately, the tensions between (and within) our neighborhood young men will not be resolved until the larger issues of family, race, and economics are addressed. That is the character of violence: it is *always* both personal and political, as we try to show repeatedly in this volume.

To secure peace with justice, whether locally or globally, requires that peacemakers assume a double stance. On one hand, we must be close enough to a given conflict that we can identify the particularities of each party and situation, which calls for the approach of community organizers, social workers and pastors. On the other hand, we also need to step back enough to see the influence of larger historical, social, and ideological forces, requiring the skills of social analysis and advocacy. Holistic peacemaking cannot ignore any of these competences or perspectives if it is to be transformative. And if we do not experiment with alternatives, we are left with the retributive solutions of sheriffs and the prison system, which merely manage the inevitable conflicts generated by a dysfunctional society.

We narrate our neighborhood incident not because it is a success story, but because it is a case in point. The same dynamics are inscribed in countless episodes of private abuse and public violation spread across the social landscapes of North America, and are writ large across global geopolitics, from Iraq to Myanmar to Colombia. Indeed, the human family as a whole is increasingly hostage to what Dr. King identified as a "descending spiral of violence." To further explore this, we do well to turn to a classic little book entitled *Spiral of Violence* (1971), written by a contemporary of King's and a fellow apostle of nonviolence, Dom Helder Camara.

Camara, the late Catholic archbishop of Recife, Brazil, was one of the original animators of liberation theology. He moved out of his opulent manse and lived among the *favelas* in order to see close up the violence of grinding poverty that was crippling his country. "When I give food to the poor, they call me a saint," Camara famously said, "but when I ask why the poor have no food, they call me a Communist." The political landscape of the 1960s all over the Third World, not least in Latin America, was marked by revolutionary insurgent groups who were battling violently repressive military dictatorships. Unlike many other ethicists and theologians working during this period, Camara was not content with moral condemnations of the armed insurgencies rising all over the Third

World, though he was deeply committed to nonviolence. *Spiral of Violence* attempts to understand the genesis of violence in order to know how and where to intervene and interrupt it.[1]

Camara's experience taught him that the various forms of violence plaguing communities of the poor—from addiction and crime to rioting and guerilla warfare—were all reactions to fundamental experiences of injustice and violation. He called these "Violence #1." In Brazil, the foremost factor was structural poverty, such as the radical disparity in land ownership between the elites and the majority of *campesinos*; foreign corporations logging the rainforests while driving indigenous people off their lands; the long-standing racism toward Afro-Brazilians; and First World arms sales that propped up a military dictatorship. Such "generative conditions" include lack of social opportunity, educational discrimination, police harassment, linguistic suppression, unemployment, military occupation, and so on. Typically, the conditions of Violence #1 are woven into the fabric of society and thus are widely accepted as "normal," "inevitable," or "beyond our capacity to change." But human beings sooner or later react to violation, Camara argued.

"Violence #2," best described psychologically as rage, is a response to the sometimes invisible, sometimes inscrutable, but always *felt* conditions of Violence #1. These reactions vary in their scope and target. *Introjected* rage results in, for example, teen suicide, addictions of all kinds, even eating disorders and depression. When *projected* outward, it is usually toward what is closest at hand—think of the classic scenario in which someone who has just been laid off at work comes home and kicks the dog in frustration. Thus the next level of victim is usually in the family, neighborhood, or workplace; the presenting symptoms are spousal abuse, family abandonment, petty crime, gangbanging, bar fights, school shootings, job truancy, and so on. In fewer cases, violence is turned outward against the institutions that either sponsored the oppression or did nothing to undo it. Only when there is a measure of political consciousness concerning Violence #1 does this become organized into urban uprisings, bread riots, so-called social banditry of the Robin Hood type, or full-blown armed insurgency or guerilla warfare.

Generally people who do not feel the effects of Violence #1—First

---

1. Published in English in 1971, the book has inexplicably been long out of print. It is, however, available online at www.alastairmcintosh.com/general/spiral-of-violence.htm. Camara was a pastor, poet, and activist, and published a dozen books. Despite the fact that he is widely regarded as one of the most influential churchmen of the twentieth century, there is no major biography of Camara available in English; the most definitive work in Portuguese is Piletti and Praxedes (1997). For an anthology of his writings, see McDonagh (2009). For broader background on the era, see Klaiber (1998).

World suburbanites, for example, or elites the world over—do not experience the effects of Violence #2 either. Until, that is, it becomes well advanced, as in the Los Angeles uprising of 1992, or the 2001 attacks on the World Trade Center. This is why insulated people of privilege typically respond to reports (or anecdotal experiences) of Violence #2 with comments such as:

- "Those gang members should be locked up!"
- "That rioting was just the work of a few malcontents"; or
- "The guerillas are all Communist subversives sponsored by Cuba!"

Unfortunately, restorative justice workers responding to criminal behavior are mobilizing at the point of Violence #2, usually without inquiring about the conditions that may have generated it. Indeed, some facilitators insist that only the presenting incident is relevant to the process, and protest that they "can't take on the larger social issues." But this kind of approach, as Zehr and Toews acknowledge, is "too individualized or astructural, ignoring or even perpetuating social problems" (2004: ix).

James Gilligan, a medical psychiatrist who directed the Center for the Study of Violence at Harvard Medical School, argues:

Any approach to a theory of violence needs to begin with a look at the structural violence of this country. . . . By "structural violence" I mean the increased rates of death and disability suffered by those who occupy the bottom rungs of society, as contrasted with the relatively lower death rates experienced by those who are above them. *Structural* violence causes far more deaths than *behavioral* violence. (1997: 191, 195)

"The most effective and powerful stimulus of violence in the human species is the experience of shame and humiliation," Gilligan explains (Ibid.: 223). "It is not lack of material things that causes shame, it is the gap or disparity between the wealth and income of those on the top and those at the bottom of the social hierarchy" (Ibid.: 201).

Neither Camara nor Gilligan are trying to exonerate perpetrators of Violence #2 from moral responsibility. Structural violence does not *justify* reactive violence, but it does make it *inevitable*. Equally predictable in the spiral is Violence #3—the counterreaction of those in power to the rage of the marginalized, the antisocial, or the subversive. The reactive violence of crime or insurgency must be quelled by the far superior force of the police or the military. Examples would be: arresting the abused wife who attacked her husband; police violently breaking up a demonstration; or the U.S. occupation of Iraq. Violence #3 is usually viewed by the comfortable classes as acceptable, moral, and necessary to preserve law and order. Criminals or rebels using guns are wrong, but officers or soldiers using the same guns are justified, even heroic. Violence #3 is usually swift, severe, and often final, whether it is expressed in gang sweeps, the death penalty, or military "Shock and Awe." If restorative justice advocates err by responding only at the level of Violence #2, peace activists err by typically mobilizing only in the face of the threat, or after the fact, of Violence #3.

The end result of Violence #3 is the intensification of the conditions of Violence #1. Examples would be "get tough on crime" legislation and the growing prison industrial complex in the United States; economic structural adjustment and currency devaluation in Argentina; or counter-insurgency warfare in Colombia. Camara and Gilligan both advocate that peacemakers seek to intervene at the point of *structural* violence, rather than waiting until presenting symptoms of *behavioral* violence become intolerable.

Two personal examples further illustrate this model (below, figure 1.1). In our former neighborhood in East Los Angeles, first generation immigrant Latino young men told us that teachers expected less from them and counseled them exclusively to be construction workers or service industry employees. Their schools were underresourced, and these boys didn't have the personal funds to buy computers. On the street they were profiled by police and hounded by gang members. Their fantasy was to make it out of the *barrio* by being a sports star; their reality was drugs and crime. This was the face of Violence #1 in our neighborhood.

We knew kids who felt powerless and ashamed because they were failing in school and couldn't get a job. Some started selling drugs because that was the only way they believed they could make money. A few joined gangs and started packing guns for both protection and prestige. This was the typical scenario of Violence #2. Arrest and jail inevitably followed, where these young men were exposed to more degradation and turf fights (Violence #3). Once out of prison, they found it even more difficult to get a job because of their record and were thus likely to continue into more serious crime, addiction, and rage (intensification of Violence #1). We cite these examples because while the model is abstract, our intimate experience with our neighbors was poignant and painful.

The 1992 Los Angeles Uprising—the largest civil disturbance in the history of the United States and equally close in our experience—provides a political corollary. In the summer of 1965, the Watts neighborhood exploded in the first of a series of urban uprisings in that decade, reacting to patterns of racism, poverty, and police abuse. Watts was poor in part because of a long history of segregation and in part because city planners dismantled the rapid transit system, which residents used to go to work, and instead built freeways *through* their neighborhoods. Industrial flight left the community further ravaged by layoffs and unemployment (Violence #1). These patterns continued to plague the African American community until April 1992, when four white police officers were acquitted by a white suburban jury in the beating of black motorist Rodney King, famously captured on video. This was the last straw of indignity for many African Americans; the percolating rage boiled over (Violence #2).

Three days of looting and burning saw more than fifty persons killed and millions of dollars worth of property torched. Ched was on the streets with other community activists trying to "keep the peace while standing for justice"—one of many grassroots neighborhood peacekeeping efforts around the city (see Myers, 1994: 45ff.). The counterreaction, as in 1965, was for the National Guard to occupy economically marginalized sections of Los Angeles for several days (Violence #3). Young, poor blacks and Latinos were scapegoated for the rioting, and tougher policing, racial profiling, and draconian sentencing guidelines followed. There was renewed flight to the suburbs, further hollowing out the affected neighborhoods (intensification of Violence #1).

Figure 1.1

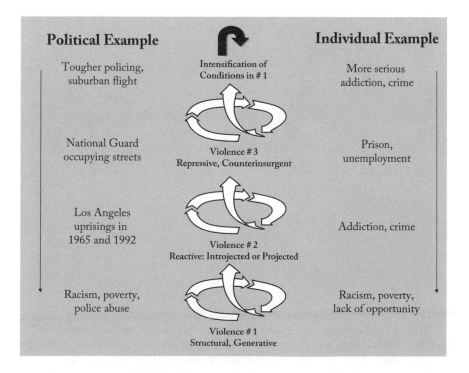

This model illuminates the whole cycle of violence from domestic abuse to international armed conflict.[2] It challenges us to find appropriate strategies of peacemaking and violence reduction at each stage, even as we diligently work "upstream" to find the headwaters of violence. Ultimately *every* violation is predicated upon an unequal exercise or distribution of economic, social, political, or personal power (Violence #1). True justice, therefore, must ensure that the relationships being "restored" are ones in which power is redistributed *more* equitably than before. The spiral of violence model encourages us to do careful structural analysis of specific violations we are dealing with and of the social context in which we are working.

---

2. There are ideological aspects to the spiral as well, rationalizations that are used to justify each level of violence. Walter Wink has analyzed these as "myths of redemptive violence," and we refer the reader to his excellent discussion (1992: 13ff.).

2

TENDING THE BRANCHES
OF PEACEMAKING

We who advocate restorative justice are . . . obligated to have our
eyes wide open, to listen to our critics, to balance our visions against
realities. Indeed, we must be both advocates and critics. We must
practice two fundamental values of restorative justice: respect and
humility.

—Zehr and Toews (2004: ix)

The genealogy of virtually every contemporary North American expression of nonviolence and conflict transformation can be traced through three great social movements in the middle part of the twentieth century: Gandhi's experiments with *satyagraha* in the Indian independence movement;[1] the civil rights movement for racial and economic justice in the United States (see Harding, 1990); and the establishment of the United Nations as an international peacekeeping institution.[2] Each of these three historic initiatives raised hopes in progressive circles that even the most protracted civil and national conflicts could be addressed through nonviolent means.

These streams influenced North American antiwar movements in the 1960s and '70s, as well as those exploring how nonviolent tools might resolve interpersonal and community conflicts. From the 1980s on there was a blossoming of mediation, conflict resolution, nonviolent communication, and nascent restorative justice practices.[3] At the same time, other activists were experimenting with nonviolent international peacekeeping,

---

1. Recommended introductions are Gandhi (1954); Juergensmeyer (1984); Bondurant (1971); and Merton (1965).

2. For a history and an overview, see Rubinstein (2008) and Schlesinger (2003).

3. See, e.g., Fisher, Ury, and Patton (1991); Rosenburg (1999); Schrock-Shenk and Ressler (1999); Bush and Folger (1994); and Zehr (1990 and 2002).

violence reduction efforts in war zones, and peace-building diplomacy. Still others were continuing to use methods of nonviolent direct action to address militarism and social injustice of all kinds, such as opposition to nuclear power and weapons, farmworkers' and other poor peoples' struggles for civil and economic rights, and environmental issues.[4]

Although all of these movements are branches of the same historic tree of peacemaking, it is our perception that over the last quarter century they have grown apart from one another. Divergences have become institutionalized and in some cases even professionalized, with little communication between the camps. To illustrate this we point to our own experience.

2A. Estranged Relatives:
Mediation and Nonviolent Action

We met at a peacemaking conference in 1997 at which both of us were speaking.[5] After sitting in on each other's sessions, we began an ongoing dialogue concerning how best to mitigate violence in our society. We discovered that our respective worlds—Elaine's among mediators and restorative justice facilitators, Ched's among nonviolent activists—were surprisingly segregated. Our circles tended to keep a wary, and not always respectful, distance and rarely talked to each other. While both camps share much of the same analysis around the epidemic of violence, they spin in different orbits, each thinking that *their* nonviolent skill set is most effective. In retrospect, we marvel at how insulated we were from the strength, perspective, and insight of each other's practices.

At the time we met, Ched had worked for twenty years in the field of active nonviolence, involving a wide variety of peace and justice campaigns, from disarmament to immigrant rights and from community organizing to international solidarity. He had participated in different forms of direct action and "public liturgy" (see Kellermann, 1991), including civil disobedience, boycotts, sanctuary refugee smuggling, and labor strikes. Ched had collegial relationships with local, regional, and national organizations, and had taught and trained in the theology and politics of nonviolence. Yet he could count on one hand the times he had talked at length, much less collaborated with, someone in the restorative justice or conflict transformation field.

---

4. For introductions to twentieth-century nonviolence movements in North America and abroad, see Powers and Vogele (1997); Lynd and Lynd (1995); Cooney and Michalowski (1987); and Sharp (1973).

5. This section is an edited version of an article that appeared in *Mennonite Conciliation Quarterly*, Winter 2002, pp. 4-6.

During his decade as a regional program director for the American Friends Service Committee, Ched was vaguely aware of Victim-Offender Reconciliation projects and Creative Conflict Resolution programs, and knew that the field of peace studies was growing rapidly. But as an activist, he was suspicious that academic programs were overly insular and theoretical, and that mediators tended to paper over issues of social power and political structures in order to achieve "resolution." He had learned from Gandhi that the first task of genuine nonviolence was to unmask injustice, which usually meant *invoking* conflict so the truth would be revealed (see volume I, chapter 2). Yet Ched had never sat in on an actual mediation!

Elaine's experience was the mirrored opposite. For more than a decade she had facilitated countless victim-offender cases, managed a local VORP (Victim Offender Reconciliation Program; see below pp. 47-48), interacted regularly with the criminal justice system, taught at the Center for Peacemaking and Conflict Studies at Fresno Pacific University, and provided mediation services for churches, schools, and businesses. Despite having studied Gandhi and King, however, she had no working relationship with groups engaged in nonviolent direct action; indeed, she perceived public protest as sometimes unconstructive and polarizing. Her mediation culture emphasized process and stressed the importance of not taking sides in a conflict. But Elaine began to question whether mediators can really be neutral or equal advocates for both parties in a situation of clear oppression or injustice. And she noticed that many colleagues were failing to include a contextual power analysis in their approach to a conflict, and thus weren't giving adequate attention to inequities in the scenario and the process (see below, chapter 3).

Elaine observed a tendency among mediators to focus on interpersonal dynamics to the exclusion of structural ones, leading some practitioners to believe that they "can mediate anything." This doesn't acknowledge that often conflicts are rooted in difficult underlying issues such as race, class, or gender. Also problematic is the fact that many practices of mediation depend directly or indirectly on coercive power. Much victim offender dialogue work, for example, is predicated upon the sanctioning power of the criminal justice system, in which the alternative to mediation is punishment.

Ched, in turn, acknowledged that activists often forget that dialogue is supposed to be both the beginning *and* ending point of nonviolent engagement. Direct action is called for only when other conciliatory measures are consistently ignored and one's legitimate demands silenced. Following Gandhi, Martin Luther King knew that his nonviolent campaigns to disrupt the "good order" of Jim Crow relied on interpretive strategies that sought to advance public conversation and consciousness, so that old worldviews and social patterns could be transformed. Dr. King's powerful public oratory was thus the dialogical counterpart to freedom marches, bus boycotts, and lunch counter sit-ins. Indeed, the goal of nonviolent action is to coerce one's adversary back to the table so that differences can be *mediated*, power equalized, and peace negotiated. Gandhi and King both insisted that the adversary ultimately had to be part of the solution. Ched realized that too much contemporary activism turns to street protest before dialogue has even been attempted and without a plan (or the skills!) for pursuing a negotiated outcome when the time is right.

We thus came to believe that activists need to think more about how to get people to the table, while mediators need to wrestle with what should happen if and when conversation breaks down or is impossible because of power imbalances. Our concern is to reintegrate and interrelate all of the different practices of peacemaking in order to combat the functional balkanization that exists between us. Our first opportunity to open up this conversation was at the Christian Peacemaker Teams congress in 1998, where we proposed that nonviolent action and mediation, though "estranged," were in fact relatives. We expressed the hope that our faith communities might be willing and able to weave back together the fraying fabric of restorative justice and peacemaking in North America. That conversation has, over the last decade, evolved into this book.

The problem is not so much outright rivalry between our two camps as it is benign neglect toward, and ignorance of, each other's strengths. We do, however, get strident and parochial about our areas of focus and expertise. "*This* is the true model of family group conferencing!" "Nonviolence requires *this* kind of action!" Such passion is a vocational hazard for those involved in politics and religion—and many of us are drawing on both realms! Those of us with roots in the Christian tradition know all too well how pronouncements of orthodoxy are not only impotent to build the church, but often instrumental in fragmenting it. In our polarized society there is already too much public debate (a verb that tellingly stems from the French *débattre*, meaning "to batter"). Differences are important, of course, and a given point of view must be argued (from the Latin *arguere*, "to make clear"). The problem arises when our rhetoric deteriorates into reiterations of our position without listening to the other (significantly, the frequentative form of *arguere* means "to babble" or "to chatter"). What is needed instead is the discipline of conversation (from the Middle English *conversen* meaning "to associate with"; also from the Latin *conversus*, meaning "a turning around"). Conversation is a discourse that holds within it the possibility of mutual conversion.

We think the fragmentation among the various branches of the peacemaking tree is counterindicative to what we ought to be doing in a world groaning under the weight of violence and violation of every kind. We each have a responsibility to stay in conversation with other disciplines, to help weave back together the frayed tapestry of restorative justice and peacemaking. We are aware that some of our colleagues would, conversely, prefer to see their practices become more narrowly specialized and professionalized.[6] Nevertheless, in this book we contend that we need to broaden the parameters and deepen the foundations of our respective restorative justice and peacemaking work, while embracing the nonviolent experiments of others. To help us think more "ecumenically" in this way, we offer the following model, which articulates a continuum of peacemaking strategies that vary according to context and/or stages of a conflict, but which are interlocking and interdependent.

2B. Full-Spectrum Peacemaking

At the outset we wish to surface an important distinction, which is more than semantic. Generally in peacemaking thought, "conflict" is a broad term referring to parties who are at odds, and that can apply to both personal and political disputes, and to both nonviolent and violent scenarios. "Violation," however, is a distinct subset of conflict, occurring when one party acts wittingly or unwittingly to dominate another, directly through violence or systemically through injustice.

A conflict can range from a sharp difference of opinion to an act of war between nations. Not all conflict involves violation, but all violation is conflictual. Violation is when a drunk driver kills a young woman, or a man kidnaps and murders a seven-year-old girl (below, chapter 4). A plane being flown intentionally into a building killing thousands or a political splinter group in Iraq kidnapping and murdering a peace worker (below, chapter 5) are both violations within the context of the wider political conflict of war. A homeless person dying on the streets of Atlanta (below, 6B) or a historic massacre of Native Americans by the U.S. Cavalry being referred to in official narratives as a "battle" (below, 7A) are violations resulting from structural injustice, not just group conflict.

Conflict is often—but violation is *always*—rooted in personal or political disparities of power or justice.[7] This is why we have bracketed this chapter

---

6. For example, some have pled with us not to "dilute" or "distract" the increasingly technical field of victim-offender facilitation by including such practices as truth and reconciliation or violence reduction in war zones under the rubric of restorative justice. Similarly, many nonviolent activist colleagues remain unconvinced that the field of restorative justice has anything to bring to their work.

7. Schrock-Shenk and Ressler recognize the distinction we are making here in their useful definitions: "Conflict is a disagreement between interdependent people; it is the perception of incompatible or mutually exclusive needs or goals. . . . Power and its use and abuse is always a significant factor when conflict goes awry or turns violent. When

with a recognition of the complex social factors involved in the spiral of violence (above, chapter 1) and a discussion about mapping power and privilege (below, chapter 3).[8] Our focus in this book is on violating conflict, which is more difficult to address than a dispute over differences. Thus restorative justice and peacemaking work, as we stipulated in our introduction, draws on "a range of nonviolent responses to injustice, violation, and/or violence" in order to "determine how to make things as right as possible" between victims, offenders, and their communities. Let us now look at that range.

There are two distinct vectors that define conflict scenarios. One is whether the parties in struggle are able and willing to be in conversation at all. The other is whether or not there is a third party involved in helping address and resolve the conflict. The vertical axis in figure 2.1 distinguishes between *cooperative* (right side) and *noncooperative* (left side) scenarios. The horizontal axis, in turn, indicates *third party* involvement (above) or absence (below).

Within this grid are four basic strategies of conflict transformation:

1. **Negotiation** requires relative equity and trust between the persons or groups in conflict, as well as a willingness and an ability to articulate one's own interests, to listen to the other's, to find common ground, and to practice the art of compromise. In fact, we routinely resolve disputes in our daily lives (at home, in the neighborhood, and at the workplace) through negotiation, most often in an informal and ad hoc manner. Negotiation is the ideal form of conflict transformation, but in the real world of power disparities, it is not always possible.

2. Moving counterclockwise around the quadrants the conflict scenario intensifies. **Mediation/facilitated dialogue** is used when parties are *not* able to work things out themselves, usually because trust has broken down (mediation) or because power is so unevenly distributed

---

someone, or a group of someones, has been silenced or victimized, the conflict is no longer a neutral one or simply 'differences with tension'" (1999: 23f.). In volume I we stipulate this distinction in our reading of Matthew 18—Jesus' exhortations there address not just conflict, but violation (chapter 3).

8. We emphasize violation as a subset of conflict because in some restorative justice circles that deal with crime, there is a tendency to apply the dynamics of "conflict mediation" to the process between victims and offenders, parties who have (in most cases) only "met" through violation. We prefer to reserve the term "mediation" for the work of resolving differences between relatively equal parties, while victim-offender work is best described as "facilitated dialogue" (reflected in the second quadrant of the model below). It is our concern in this work to highlight the too-often obscured backdrop of power and the nature of social systems that usually mean that the offender is also a victim, and the victim often also an offender (in the sense of race, class, or gender privilege, for example).

Figure 2.1

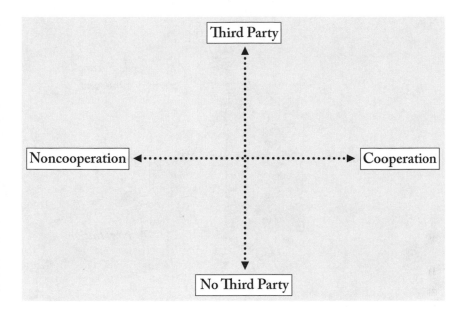

between them that one party does not feel safe meeting with the other party alone or does not believe they will be heard (dialogue). The parties are, however, willing to collaborate in finding a resolution. A trusted or professional third party is thus invited in to help them talk to each other and come up with their own agreements to solve the conflict or violation (the mediator or facilitator is *not* a decision maker in this process; figure 2.2). The art of mediation/dialogue is ancient among human communities, with many different cultural expressions, and has been revived in the contemporary restorative justice movement.

3. Now we move from a cooperative to a noncooperative scenario, in which parties are unwilling or unable to come to the table with each other. The upper left quadrant is usually called **arbitration**. Either the parties empower, or an outside authority appoints, an independent adjudicator to decide how to resolve the conflict. The parties narrate their experience and needs, but the adjudicator decides. This is, of course, the architecture of the western legal system where plaintiffs and defendants argue their cases and a judge or jury decides on the merits of the case.

4. The worst-case scenario is when conflict is raging with no third party able to arbitrate because of intense hostility or open warfare between the parties. In this quadrant, **coercion** is the default, with the stronger party normally prevailing.

Figure 2.2

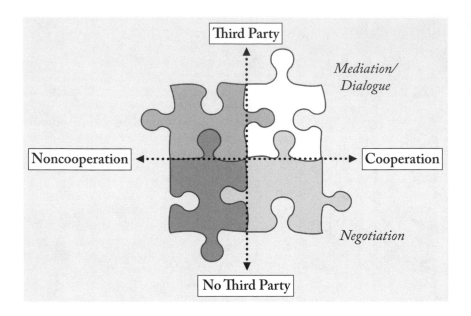

This model is normally used to describe interpersonal conflict and, from a broader restorative justice and peacemaking standpoint, needs some revision and elaboration. For example, both negotiation and mediation have political expressions, which tend to be more formal and shaped by rules and protocols. Negotiation is used routinely to resolve conflicts between institutions (e.g., labor and management) or between national bodies (e.g., trade or environmental disputes), while **third-party diplomacy** is a form of mediation, such as that offered by U.N. representatives in member nation conflicts.

In the third quadrant, arbitration doesn't do justice to the spectrum of strategies that can involve third party intervention in a conflict. The work of **international peacekeeping** should be included here, such as when two groups in armed conflict agree to (or are forced as condition of a truce to accept) a UN peacekeeping force.[9] **Truth and Reconciliation** work—the attempt to adjudicate historic injustice and to facilitate steps toward overcoming long-standing alienation—also belongs here. We will have more to say on this below (2C).

---

9. See Crocker, Hampson, and Aall (2007); Daniel and Hayes (1995); and www.un .org/Depts/dpko/dpko/index.asp. Related is the work of the UN Peacebuilding Commission, which attempts to build confidence and dialogue in "post-conflict recovery" (www. un.org/peace/peacebuilding/mandate.shtml).

Nor should the fourth quadrant be conceded to the law of the jungle—particularly because this is the context in which so many oppressed people around the world live. The persistence of intolerable conditions is, of course, used to justify both revolutionary armed struggle and state warmaking. But such circumstances have also given birth to the great nonviolent resistance movements of the twentieth century. **Nonviolent Coercion** is thus the alternative to taking up a gun in this scenario of last resort. Tactics range from passive non-cooperation (e.g., boycotts, strikes, and refusal of orders) to active resistance (e.g., sit-ins, nonviolent sabotage, and civil disobedience).[10] Nonviolent struggle is designed to unmask injustice, impede continuing oppression, and exert moral pressure on the adversary to negotiate social and political change (figure 2.3).

Figure 2.3

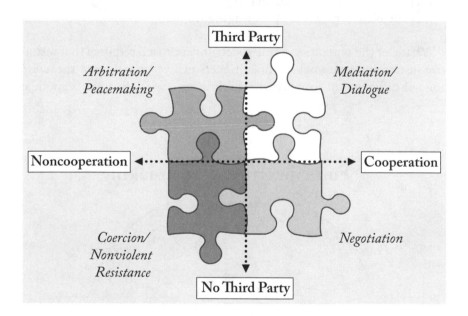

A "full-spectrum" approach contends that restorative justice and peacemaking work, broadly and inclusively defined, can be plotted on a *continuum* around these four quadrants. The best strategy is always preventative, addressing the roots of violence by attending to personal patterns and political structures of injustice. When violation and conflict do occur,

---

10. See especially the classic three-volume work of Gene Sharp (1973), as well as his work on nonviolent civilian national defense. The Public Broadcasting Service's documentary on nonviolent movements is also a useful primer: see www.aforcemorepowerful.org.

however, our task is to try to intervene in the spiral of violence as soon as possible. And whichever quadrant we find ourselves beginning in, our aim should be to move the process steadily clockwise around the circle: de-escalating the conflict, empowering victims, and calling offenders and aggressors to accountability. Ideally, every conflict should be resolved in the first quadrant, where the parties can self-determine a just outcome. But the model reminds us that when and if this is not possible, there are *always* nonviolent alternatives to the pathologies of oppression, reactive violence, and retribution.

Ted Lewis, a mediator and restorative justice colleague in Eugene, Oregon, suggested we rename the four quadrants thus:

1. Negotiation is **Peacebuilding**;
2. Mediation/Dialogue is **Peacemaking**;
3. Arbitration, etc. is **Peacekeeping**;
4. Nonviolent struggle is **Peacewaging** (figure 2.4).

Whatever the semantics, a full-spectrum approach requires that restorative justice and peacemaking practitioners utilize or call upon the *whole* range of different but complementary skill sets. Specialization is good, as

Figure 2.4

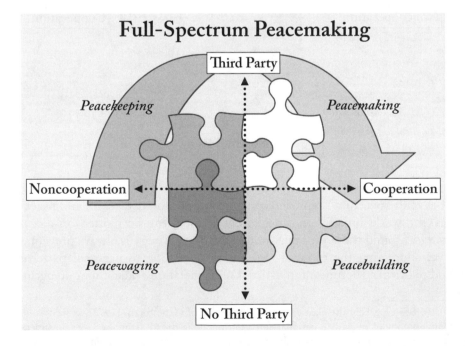

Full-Spectrum Peacemaking

Third Party

Peacekeeping   Peacemaking

Noncooperation ◄┈┈┈┈┈┈┈┈┈┈┈┈► Cooperation

Peacewaging   Peacebuilding

No Third Party

long as we know the strengths and limits of our particular approach, and are committed to referring out to or calling upon the competences of others. To do this well, we will have to overcome our balkanization.

2C. Moral Imagination and Social Change

Again we emphasize how important it is to take into account issues of power in all quadrants. One issue is the differential in personal or social power among parties, which has a profound impact even on the "cooperative" side of the spectrum. There are real differences between spouses negotiating and a student leader trying to negotiate with a university president, or a homeless activist with a chief of police. Genuine negotiation requires relative equity and/or fundamental respect between parties. Indeed, stronger parties rarely negotiate with weaker ones unless they are politically or morally compelled. The same may be said for mediation and facilitated dialogue, which we address further in the next chapter.

An even thornier issue is the relationship of restorative strategies to institutions (especially state or corporate) that wield retributive power. When government representatives "negotiate" by joining their proposals with economic or military threats, this is not true negotiation, but a veiled strategy of coercion. Questions of power are particularly acute when it comes to mediation/facilitation. Is the third party a paid professional? If so, who is footing the bill? Is she or he a direct or indirect agent of social or political authority, such as a tribal government, a criminal justice system, or the U.N. Security Council? Are one or both parties coming to mediation in a voluntary or a mandated capacity?[11] With international mediation such as in the case of the Israel/Palestine conflict, the civilian conciliation work of John Paul Lederach is different in character than the quasi-governmental diplomacy of Jimmy Carter, which is in turn different from the U.S. State Department's attempts to broker "peace deals."[12]

The same concerns pertain to the "noncooperative" side of the spectrum. In traditional communities, conflicted parties will often ask a trusted friend or leader to settle a dispute apart from any sanctioning authority. In the West, however, arbitration is more often associated with a person (e.g., a judge) or an institution (e.g., the World Trade Organization) that wields social-political power. Professional, legal, and governmental arbitration

---

11. Victim-offender dialogue in a criminal justice context is a case in point: the offender is often there by mandate from a judge or probation officer. A process ordered by a court will obviously exhibit a very different power dynamic than a wholly voluntary one (see below, 3B).

12. See Lederach and Jenner (2002); Carter (2006).

is regulated by protocols, which theoretically safeguard the rights of both parties. The same is not the case, however, when it comes to international peacekeeping. The United Nations' "Blue Helmet" forces represent a noble experiment with transnational policing in a world still ruled by the politics of sovereignty (Armengal, 1995). Unfortunately, in recent years this has been compromised by U.S. efforts to cloak its foreign intervention and regime-change strategies with UN legitimation. U.S. soldiers in the current occupation of Iraq are *not* peacekeepers, however much their mission may include policing or mitigation of factional fighting; insofar as these forces are under U.S. command and control, they are an arm of U.S. military/foreign policy.[13]

With the atrophy of genuine international policing, some groups have begun experimenting with **nonviolent civilian peacekeeping** efforts. This includes Christian Peacemaker Teams standing between Israeli tanks and Palestinian stone throwers; Witness for Peace's accompaniment of refugees through war zones in Central America; and the Nonviolent Peace Force's work in Sri Lanka.[14] This is a hopeful, if risky and demanding, new field of experimentation. We should also include in this vein experiments in domestic grassroots violence-reduction work, such as the gang truce work of Aqeela Sherrills and others in Los Angeles.[15]

Truth and reconciliation processes, too, exhibit profound differences depending on their relation to state power. The South African Truth and Reconciliation Commission, for example, had the authority both to subpoena and to prosecute, while the Greensboro Truth and Community Reconciliation Project, a victim-initiated, grassroots process, relied on moral persuasion and community organizing (below, 7B). TRCs are an exciting innovation in adjudicating and healing historical conflict; but it makes a difference whether they are coming from "above" or "below" (see Kim, Kollontai, and Hoyland, 2008; Daye, 2004). Even nonviolent coercion is

---

13. This can be seen, for example, by U.S. reactions to UN criticisms of its operations in Iraq (see, e.g., Tyler, 2004).

14. See www.cpt.org/ (below, 5B); www.witnessforpeace.org/; www.nonviolentpeaceforce .org/.

15. Sherrills, of the Community Self-Determination Institute, helped broker the 1992 truce between the Bloods and the Crips (see his story at www.theforgivenessproject.com/ stories/aqeela-sherrills-calvin-hodges). There is a compelling connection between the L.A. gang truce and the United Nations. Ralph Bunche was the highest ranking African American in the United Nations (1947-1971), and the first black Nobel Laureate, which was awarded for his brokering of the Rhodes Armistice between Israel and Egypt in 1949 (Urquhart, 1998; see also www.ralphbunche.com/). In 1992 former gang member Anthony Perry discovered the Rhodes Armistice in a University of Southern California library, and used that document, drafted by Bunche, as the basis for the truce between the Bloods and the Crips (see www.galeschools.com/black_history/bio/bunche_r.htm).

Figure 2.5

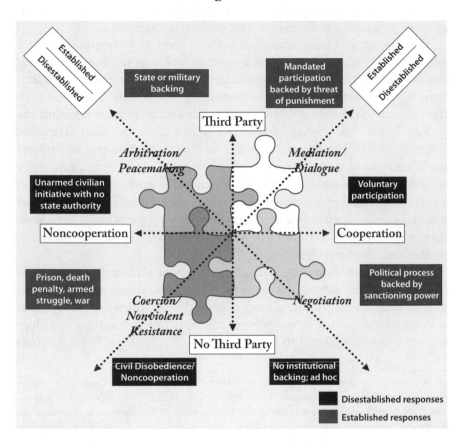

different if wielded by the state. For example, economic sanctions are some-times championed as an alternative to war. The reality in international poli-tics, however, is that sanctions are inevitably a punitive strategy employed by a stronger entity to isolate a weaker one, for example, the United States and Cuba or the United Nations and Iraq (see von Sponeck, 2006). In a world in which warfare is increasingly economic, such strategies are hardly restorative.

With these concerns in mind, therefore, we want to introduce one more important nuance to this model: distinguishing between strategies that are allied with or sponsored by institutions of coercion, and those that are not. We might call these "established" and "disestablished" trajectories, a dif-ference that takes on increasing significance as we move counterclockwise around the quadrants (figure 2.5). In order to be transparent about our "tendency" in this book, we identify as noted with the Anabaptist tradi-tion of Christianity, especially its historic commitments to radical discipleship, to biblical justice and nonviolence, and to noncooperation with all forms of state domination.[16] This orientation makes us reticent about strategies that ultimately rely on state-authorized sanctions.

This dilemma is particularly acute for restorative justice practitioners working with the criminal justice system. There is no question in our minds that victim-offender dialogue, family group conferencing, and sentencing circles represent far more humane and relational processes than the prosecutorial legal tradition, and thus should be promoted within the system. In the end, however, restorative justice advocates must determine whether (or to what degree) they are seeking to represent a transforming *alternative* to the system's core philosophy of retribution, or merely a subsidiary *complement* that attempts to make the criminal justice system a little kinder and gentler where and when possible.[17] The same question must be pressed upon political peacemaking initiatives: is our goal to *abolish* the war system, or to offer important but finally ancillary *diversions*, such as conscientious objection?[18]

This is not a question of *effect*; our best restorative justice and peacemaking work may or may not generate enough social and political inertia to transform institutions. It is one of *intent*: What will we settle for? This is not a new dilemma in our movements, but how we approach it does influence our tactical and strategic choices.[19] While this is not a question

---

16. A *tendency* is defined by Merriam-Webster as "a direction or approach toward a place, object, effect, or limit," and as "a proneness to a particular kind of thought or action." The Anabaptist movement emerged as the radical wing of the Protestant Reformation; its ecclesial progeny include the "Peace Churches"—Mennonites, Quakers, and Brethren. For good introductions to the Anabaptist tradition see Bender (1944); Weaver (1987); Estep (1996); and Williams (1999). Elaine comes from an ethnic Mennonite community in Canada and continues to embrace that tradition, though not uncritically. Throughout his adult life Ched has leaned theologically toward Anabaptism while working ecumenically, and only joined the Mennonite Church in 2008.

17. On this see Johnstone (2002: 8) and Zehr and Toews (2004).

18. A young John F. Kennedy made an interesting comment on this question shortly before the end of World War II: "War will exist until that distant day when the conscientious objector enjoys the same reputation and prestige that the warrior does today." It is cited in Douglass (2008: 6), an important new book that argues that Kennedy was killed by forces in the U.S. military-industrial-security complex that were furious at the president's genuine moves to dismantle Cold War hostilities.

19. It also mirrors the central theological and political quandary of the Anabaptist tradition. Were sixteenth-century radical reformers trying to live *without* and even *against* the state, or were they simply trying to live as peaceably as possible *under* it? Were they anarchist visionaries or quietist sectarians? However that quandary is resolved (see Myers, 1994: 355ff.), the significant fact is that the nonviolence of sixteenth-century Anabaptists, like that of the New Testament and early church, was fashioned without recourse to, and despite lethal opposition by, state power.

for every practitioner of restorative justice and peacemaking, it *should* concern those of us who work within the Peace Church tradition. Governments, armies, prisons, and police are not theologically bound to love their enemies or to renounce retribution—in our understanding of discipleship, however, followers of Jesus *are*. We would contend, moreover, that this dilemma impinges on the nonpacifist church as well. All North American Christians live and witness today in an irrefutably post-Constantinian context, which means we cannot assume that there is substantial continuity between the values of the state and those of the gospel. For these reasons, this volume has a bias toward disestablished practices of restorative justice and peacemaking.[20]

That said, we are deeply aware that the political terrain of the real world is ambiguous. There are many points of overlap and collaboration between disestablished and established strategies across the peacemaking spectrum; indeed, all of our interviewees in part 2 pursue elements of both. This brings us to a final point: we want to acknowledge two more trajectories that are always involved in social change work. One trajectory is the way of *pragmatic reform*. Today, many labor to bring practical restorative justice and nonviolent alternatives into existing systems and institutions. Their challenge is to figure out how the moral values of victim empowerment, offender accountability, relational justice, and nonlethal conflict resolution can be made workable in the real world of bureaucratized, sclerotic, and even broken systems. The other trajectory is the way of *social movements of moral imagination*. These activists are pioneering diverse new ways to apply restorative justice and peacemaking principles to different social realms where retribution and violence hold sway, often in a manner that is dismissed by established circles as ineffective or naïve.

History suggests that movements of moral imagination are the animating force for social change. In order to realize their goals, however, these movements must eventually impact and transform existing institutions. This tends to be the work of pragmatic reformers, who step into the moral authority and political inertia created by popular movements to do the equally difficult work of effecting concrete diplomatic breakthrough, governmental change, new legislation, civil rights, economic redistribution, and so on.

---

20. We want to be clear that our leaning does not arise from a concern to maintain a putative "moral purity." Ched sadly recalls heated debates, during his tenure with the American Friends Service Committee, concerning whether staff members who communicated or collaborated with organizations that supported armed struggle were compromising the Quaker Peace Testimony. We do not believe it is possible to remain "pure" in actual political engagement, nor is anyone uncompromised in our complex world. Principled navigation of difficult terrain is the most we can hope to accomplish.

To illustrate this dialectic with one notable example, the nineteenth-century Abolitionist movement led by Harriet Tubman, Frederick Douglass, and William Lloyd Garrison cleared the moral, social, and political space to end legal slavery in the United States (see Ferrell, 2006). But it also took thousands of clergy, politicians and business leaders tirelessly lobbying and pressuring the Lincoln administration to enable the president finally to step into that space and begin the long process of dismantling American apartheid.

Once a movement is institutionalized, however—politics being the art of compromise—the original moral insights are often eroded and sometimes lost altogether. To continue with our example, this can be seen in the steady atrophy of white political will from Lincoln's 1863 Emancipation Proclamation, through Reconstruction to the *Plessy v. Ferguson* decision of the Supreme Court in 1896, which upheld the constitutionality of racial segregation for the next half century under the duplicitous rubric of "separate but equal" (see Foner, 2002). When such erosion or backlash occurs, it takes another social movement to recapture and extend the original moral vision. Thus Jim Crow had to be challenged by the civil rights movement of A. Philip Randolph, Rosa Parks, Martin Luther King, and Fannie Lou Hamer (see Branch, 1988, 1998, 2006). Then the cycle starts over: the principles of the social movement are translated into legislation—such as the Voting Rights Act of 1965 and affirmative action. But these laws either have never been fully implemented or have eroded due to backlash. Hence in our own time we stand in dire need of new social movements to animate change for racial and economic justice in the United States (see, e.g., Harding, 1990).

In the long-term struggle for change, social movements and practical reformers depend on each other to capture, sustain, and recapture crucial moral ground in society. But while these two trajectories represent halves of a dialectical truth, they are not equally recognized, respected, or resourced. Social movements typically operate on a shoestring and are always under pressure to adjust their innovative experiments to the orthodoxies of the status quo. After thirty years of "movement" advocacy, for example, restorative justice principles and practices are beginning to garner the interest and qualified support of judges, DAs, and probation officers in the criminal justice system. With this has come the inevitable tendency to narrow the conversation to issues of efficacious application, technique, and case management. While this is understandable—particularly given the myriad challenges facing a criminal justice system in crisis—we think that a solely instrumental approach to the exclusion of broader social vision is a strategic mistake. Even a Department of Justice report admits that "Values, vision, mission, and goals are the foundation of the change process

. . . without being firmly grounded in these principles . . . modification of programs or development of new programs is likely to continue old paradigms with new names" (Crowe, 2000).

We think that creative (and controversial) popular movements are crucial to the health and maturity of any society, which is why this book leans in the direction of that trajectory. Grassroots, faith-oriented restorative justice and peacemaking initiatives are like "aquifers" that recharge the "tributaries" of practical change. When problem solving is deeply grounded in moral vision, justice can flow, as the great prophet Amos put it, "like a river, and righteousness like a mighty stream" (Amos 5:24).

Gandhi called the spinning wheel his most powerful nonviolent weapon (Chakrabarti, 2000). In the spirit of "respect and humility" suggested by Zehr and Toews, we must all work more consciously to reweave an integral, inclusive, and holistic fabric of restorative justice and peacemaking. Nothing less will do in the face of the escalating spiral of violence and the dead-end logic of retribution that characterize our historical moment. And nothing less is required of ambassadors of reconciliation.

3

TESTING THE SOIL OF POWER
AND PRIVILEGE

Perhaps . . . I am the face of one of your fears. Because I am a woman,
because I am Black, because I am a lesbian, because I am myself—a
Black woman warrior poet doing my work—come to ask you: are you
doing yours?

—Audre Lorde, "Sister Outsider" (2007:41f)

Restorative justice and peacemaking are not ideals but practices, which
take place in difficult, real-world terrain. This terrain is always shaped by
historic and current inequality and violence, in which some people have
and exercise more power than others. Our analysis of both the spiral of
violence (chapter 1) and the spectrum of peacemaking strategies (chapter 2) requires us, therefore, to pay careful attention to realities of social
power. In North American society we are surrounded by powerful institutions, ideologies, and personalities, but we are not typically adept at
recognizing, naming, and challenging them. Those who would transform
social conditions and bring about a greater measure of equality and peace
must learn how to "read" patterns and practices of power, and understand
the particularities and systemic characteristics of a given context.

Our theological assumption here is that biblically, power is a gift and
a "good" to be shared equitably, not a possession to be hoarded—like the
manna of Exodus 16.[1] A fundamental vision of "enough for everyone" is
why the Hebrew prophets constantly challenged the distribution of power
in their social world and why Jesus of Nazareth located himself among the

---

1. This text offers a central "instruction" that newly liberated Israel must learn to be free
of the Domination System (Exod 16:4): the Divine gift must be gathered and distributed
in a way that ensures that no one has too much and everyone has enough (16:16ff.). This is
the key concept in what we call "Sabbath Economics" (Myers, 2001).

most marginalized. In the first volume of this project, we examine similarities between Mark's Jesus and Martin Luther King, Jr., as peacemakers who understood the need first to be "disturbers of the peace" (volume I, chapter 2). And we see how Matthew's Jesus predicates his alternative, restorative practice for adjudicating violation upon a careful analysis of relative power in the community, giving radical moral priority to the "least" (volume I, 3B). It is our further assumption, then, that Christians today should be working to promote just redistributions of power whenever and wherever needed, rather than preoccupied with increasing our own individual or group power, as the dominant culture unabashedly teaches us to do.

Sometimes the exercise of power around us is clearly evident, such as in a police sweep, a corporate takeover, a factory closing and mass layoff, the fulminations of a playground bully, or the glamorous trappings of a celebrity function. More often in daily life, however, social power is mystified, obfuscated, or denied—especially by those who have it. When a white person claims to be "color blind," or someone with a college education asserts that "we're all more or less middle class," or a man insists "I'm not sexist," there are terrains of privilege and power that are not being acknowledged. So when a bank CEO complains about how he is at the mercy of market forces, a millionaire presidential candidate tries to act folksy at a campaign barbecue, or a major oil company advertises how much it is doing for the environment, we do well to practice the "hermeneutics of suspicion." Denial of actual power makes true accountability impossible—and unaccountable power is *the* central threat to genuine political, economic, and cultural democracy. A central discipline for ambassadors of reconciliation, therefore, is our willingness and ability to apprehend critically how power is distributed in our own households and communities, in the specific political scenarios we wish to engage, and in the broader society in which we live and work.

3A. Mapping Social Power

Power is a combination of "nature" and "nurture." For the purposes of this analysis, we are defining power in social rather than psychic terms. We readily acknowledge that someone who is marginalized can exercise tremendous spiritual power, or that poor people can inwardly be deeply content; however, these are not dimensions we are focusing on here. In its social dimension, power is *always* humanly constructed and has a complex history on which prevailing intra- and intergroup relations are predicated.

Social power is difficult to get a handle on because it varies with context and, as noted, is usually unacknowledged by those who exercise it.

The Greek word *dynamis* used in the New Testament means both power and ability. This reminds us that social power can be defined generically according to a combination of four basic capacities:

- *Mobility*: the ability to be where one is "at home" and to move where one wishes;
- *Access*: the ability to procure what one needs for health and well-being;
- *Self-determination*: the ability to make the decisions that most affect one's life;
- *Influence*: the ability to be heard, seen, and respected.

The adequate realization of these capacities is often spoken of abstractly in terms of "peace," "justice," "freedom," "equal rights," and so on.

Social power must always be analyzed *in context*, and this is a multidimensional task. There are at least three basic "epistemological frameworks" through which human beings perceive their social world:[2]

1. The dominant social context. In any given society, certain structures or systems are "hegemonic," meaning that their power and influence prevails and that they are widely acknowledged as "normative" or "mainstream." These may be economic (e.g., banking systems or market mechanisms in capitalism); political (e.g., representative democracy or a legal system that privileges private property); or cultural (e.g., the commercial media or professional sports). For example, Nelson Johnson names this dominant context as the putative "culture of civility" of the Jim Crow South (below, 7B, i); Murphy Davis names a system that controls expendable populations through prisons and poverty (below, 6B, ii).

2. Specific social subsets. Within the larger sphere of "mainstream" culture are the specific contexts of a community or region. Some of these are "minority-controlled" spaces, small and large, which may represent "exceptions to the rule." Examples would be the subcultures of a labor union; a Latino working-class barrio in East Los Angeles; a historically black college; or a gay/lesbian caucus within a Quaker Yearly Meeting. Other specific contexts reflect mainstream values: for example, a Little League team, a public school, or a particular federal bureaucracy.

In either case, a specific context is always a **subset** of the dominant

---

2. The notion of "epistemic communities"—that is, social groups that share worldview, mythos, and narrative—arose from sociology of knowledge and postmodern philosophy (see, e.g., Berger and Luckmann, 1966; MacIntyre, 1985, 1989). In a reaction to the modernist assumption that we all share a rational, universally valid view of things, these currents argue that our perceptions are formed by context and tradition. In this case, we are suggesting that our personal, communal, and social contexts represent overlapping (and often conflicting) "maps" of power.

culture. It is populated by "communities of interest," which can be ethnic, vocational, recreational, and so forth—for example, Joe Avila's recovery group (below, 4A, ii) or Lawrence Hart's Cheyenne tribe (below, 7A), or the Catholic Worker movement, which has influenced several of our interviewees. Obviously, the most basic specific context is that of the family or household. These local formations usually seem more real or immediate to us than do broader categories: for example, it is more important to Ched that he is a fifth-generation Californian than a U.S. citizen; Elaine identifies more with "Mennonite" than the more general rubric "Christian." But someone whose core identity is as father and local firefighter might also identify more loosely as an "angry taxpayer," casual bluegrass picker, and despondent Cubs fan. These subsets express objective sociological patterns and conditions (e.g., all teachers at this school hold certain degrees; the Goth kids hang out at this coffee shop). But they also reflect some degree of subjective but shared group perceptions. For example, members of Atlantic Life Community would all, with Liz McAlister, embrace nonviolence as an ethic (below, 6A, ii); longtime residents of our little town of Oak View generally don't trust newcomers.

3. Individual subjects. Third, each of us views our dominant and specific contexts according to our social location, our race/class/gender/sexual identity, and our personal characteristics. How I view the world is shaped by my socialization within these different contexts, but also by my personality, physical/emotional stature, life experiences, and more. Persons raised in the same family or community can see things differently. A second-generation Japanese American woman raised in Hawaii who suffers from depression and is almost ready to retire as a teacher in San Francisco navigates a different matrix of contexts than does a sixth-generation Irish-English-German teenage boy who was abused by his uncle and has dropped out of school in Boston. The fact that James Loney is a gay Canadian Catholic (below, 5B), or that Myrna Bethke is an introverted Methodist pastor committed to New Jersey (below, 5A), figures in how they have navigated their response to the Iraq War.

These three contextual dimensions are modeled in figure 3.1 below. The challenge of "mapping" social power is factoring in both the *objective conditions* of our dominant and specific contexts, as well as the *individual and collective subjectivities* of our specific and individual contexts. We also need to understand how the power map can change as the contexts do. Three examples can serve to give flesh to this abstract diagram.

i. Elaine's identity has been deeply shaped by the subculture of German-speaking Mennonites who emigrated from Russia in the 1920s (specific context). She is also a citizen of Canada, living in the United States (dominant context). In relation to mainstream Canada, Mennonites are a relatively invisible minority, indicating less social power; they do, on the other hand, enjoy white privilege, indicating more social power. Within her (traditionally agrarian) ethnic subculture Elaine is "accomplished," having a graduate school education. But she also feels marginalized as a woman within the patriarchal traditions of the Mennonite church.

ii. A wheat farmer in Saskatchewan is a member of the Saskatchewan Wheat Pool (specific context), which in turn is shaped by the international political economy of wheat in a globalized market (dominant social context). The farmer has a successful two-thousand-acre operation, which makes him powerful—particularly from the perspective of, say, a Third World farmer. But his subjective perception is that he is too vulnerable to the fluctuating global price of wheat, and that his concerns aren't heeded by the Canadian government.

iii. An African American teacher rises to leadership within a state-wide teachers union (specific context); she negotiates with state lawmakers about school budgets and policies (dominant context). In her professional role she is clearly powerful—but in her Baptist church, because she is a woman, she still is not allowed to stand in the pulpit. And when driving through a white neighborhood at night, her map of power changes dramatically; she feels anxiety about being pulled over for "DWB" ("driving while black").

Mapping social power often is sabotaged by our North American tendency to hypersubjectivity. We all view the world from our subjective perceptions, filtered through the lens of the specific contexts with which we are most familiar and with which we identify. But this is intensified within our culture of individualism. Our subjective perceptions of power often either deny, or resign themselves to, the objective conditions present in the dominant culture. An example of *denial* would be a white male executive who perceives that affirmative action policies are hindering his career opportunities. His subjective perception refuses to see the structural privilege that his race and gender already afford him, and thus he resents any attempt to redress that inequality as an infringement on the "principle" of individual merit. An example of *resignation* would be an unemployed young Latino male in the inner city who harbors no career aspirations because the immediate conditions around him, and the messages he gets from his dominant cultural school, persuade him that he has no real prospects. His subjective perception may blind him to real opportunities, as well as to his own capacities and gifts (this is the "internalized oppression" that Harley Eagle talks about below).

The kind of power mapping we are suggesting here seeks to problematize our subjectivist tendency by holding them accountable to objective conditions in the dominant and specific cultural contexts. The white executive may *feel* "discriminated against" by affirmative-action policies, but in order to truly grasp his power he must come to terms with the social realities of white and male privilege, past and present. Conversely, the Latino youth may correctly *intuit* that he is socially marginalized, and that the dominant culture perceives him as "expendable," "lazy," or "dangerous." But by becoming critically conscious of this stereotype (rather than internalizing it), he and his friends can engage and resist that culture and channel their energies to practices that affirm their value and create opportunities.

Figure 3.1: Social Power, Perception, and Context

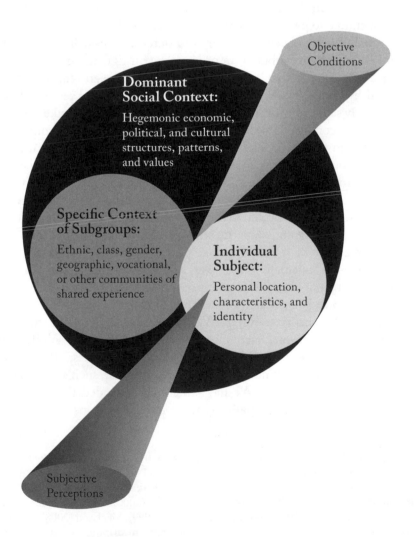

Obviously, perceptions and dynamics of power shift with the context. The Latino youth may feel powerful when hanging on the street corner with his "homies," but vulnerable and unsure when sitting in court. Similarly, the white lawyer feels powerful when in the courtroom, but vulnerable when walking down an East L.A. street at night, across from that group of homies. Part of assessing objective power is determining the ability of an individual or group to control what spaces they occupy or have access to, in order to maximize their comfort or opportunity. Thus, the businessman has many structural advantages, including the fact that he can probably ensure that he'll never walk that East L.A. street at night. The Latino youth, on the other hand, because he is unlikely to access a boardroom and finds his only power on the streets, may not be able to avoid court, due to patterns of law enforcement and racial profiling.

The goal of mapping social power is to determine how in a given context it is unequally distributed, in order to begin figuring out how every person and group in that context might have sufficient capacity to be safe, healthy, adequately resourced and mobile, heard and respected, and appropriately self-determining. In mapping power, we must take seriously both objective conditions and subjective perceptions, and find connection points between the two. Careful analysis and discernment helps us learn to transcend our personal biases and our stereotypes of others, to listen to how other groups perceive themselves and us, and to appreciate how economic and political conditions influence or determine social mobility and access. These are cross-cultural skills we need to practice, and they include self-knowledge, listening, empathy, and critical thinking.

Another aspect of mapping social power, especially for those of us who have it, is to "calculate" our power, in order to preclude our tendency toward subjective denial, and to nurture self-knowledge. The "inventory" below (figure 3.2) is a revision of existing models that are often used in antiracism and diversity trainings. We have expanded and nuanced the basic model to go beyond race, class, and gender indices.[3] While these continue to be the most important factors in power analysis, other indices are also consequential, but not often taken into account, such as reputation, physical traits, or language. We have therefore expanded the number of indices in the first column, separating them into two groups:

---

3. For how these same issues face peace and justice activists, see Myers (1994: 275ff.) and the literature cited there. More recent studies we find helpful concerning *race* include Wise (2007, 2005), Singleton and Linton (2006), Perkinson (2004), and de Leon-Hartshorne, Shearer, and Stoltzfus (2001); *gender*: Minas (2000), Enns and Myers (1999), and Johnson (2005); and *class*: hooks (2000), Roediger (1999), MacLeod (2008), and www .classism.org. For reflections on cultural considerations in mediation, see Schrock-Shenk (2000: 99ff.).

- aspects of personal or physical identity that *are not* (or not usually) the result of choices/opportunities or social conditions, for example, age, physical appearance, personality;
- aspects of personal identity that *are* (or usually are) the result of personal choices/opportunities or social conditions, for example, education, citizenship, religion.

Recognizing that social power cannot be simplistically quantified, we suggest a relative continuum from the least (1) to most powerful (4).

We have filled in the second column according to what we think the high/low spectrum is relative to the dominant culture of the United States. If you feel some resistance to our determinations, we urge you to check whether your subjective biases are obscuring objective conditions. The third column, in turn, is for the reader to work with, preferably using several different specific contexts. The different indices are interrelated and often synergistic; to be powerful in several categories is to be exponentially powerful, and conversely, to be marginalized in several categories is to be intensively marginalized. Because our self-evaluations tend to reflect subjective perception more than objective conditions, inventory work is best done in a group process. We suggest that individuals do a self-inventory, then compare notes and discuss with others in the group. Obviously, the more diverse the participants, the richer the learning.

Each of the contextual spheres discussed above need to be addressed to see how power is relative to them, and how different indices factor differently. For example, if I am a native Spanish speaker in the United States, my language will factor more powerfully in my specific context (family, barrio), but less powerfully in the dominant context (school, court). This inventory becomes most revealing if we map several different contexts. How does my power change when I shift the specific context from my own ethnic or class community to a radically different one—for example, if as a U.S. citizen I move to Zambia or Thailand as a development worker? How did Harley Eagle's power map context change when he went to work on the Pine Ridge Reservation (below, 3B)?

We believe that these models demonstrate that two axioms, often thought to contradict each other, are *both* true, and need to be held together:

1. power can be mapped; and
2. social reality is complex and variable.

We should keep in mind, as philosopher Alfred Korzybski famously said, that "the map is not the territory." Abstract models are useful only to the extent that we work honestly with them in terms of our actual lived personal and collective social terrains. Nor should they be used rigidly;

Figure 3.2: A Social Power Inventory and Worksheet for Individuals and Groups in the United States

4 = most powerful   3 = somewhat powerful   2 = not so powerful   1 = least powerful

POWER INDICES	Position (or prevailing perception) within dominant social context in United States				Specific Social Context (work, church, etc.) Estimate your level and note why			
Personal/Physical	4	3	2	1	4	3	2	1
Gender	Male			Transgender				
Race/Skin color	White			Black				
Sexual orientation	Straight			Homosexual				
Age	30-65			Under 18 or 70+				
Disability	Able			Severely disabled				
Weight	Slim			Obese				
Stature/Physical Strength	Healthy, Strong			Weak, sick				
Physical Appearance	Attractive			Unattractive				
Personality	Extrovert			Introvert				
Rational/Emotional	Rational			Emotional				
Social/Cultural/Political	4	3	2	1	4	3	2	1
Financial Assets	>$300,000			<$10,000				
Education	Graduate degree			no High School				
Marital Status	Married			Divorced				
Professional Status	Management			No title				
Religion	Protestant			Native or Muslim				
Citizenship	U.S. citizen			undocumented				
Reputation	Celebrity			Criminal				
Social Mobility	Upward			Downward				
Language/ Literacy	English			Non European				
Political Insider/ Outsider	Party position			No affiliation				
TOTAL =								

our models are simply one attempt to develop tools for the tasks facing us. Mapping social power is difficult, and neither our popular socialization nor our formal education prepares us for this kind of personal and political self-examination. We need to be patient yet persistent, probing ourselves and listening to others. But until we "do our own work," as poet Audre Lorde puts it, we won't be able to be reliable allies in restorative justice and peacemaking across the power map.

3B. Privilege in Restorative Justice Work:
A Conversation with Harley Eagle

Restorative justice practitioner Harley Eagle has a perspective on these issues that highlights why it is so important to engage social power work. Harley is enrolled in the Wapaha Ska Dakota First Nations Reserve in Saskatchewan, Canada, and resides in Winnipeg with his wife, Sue (of Russian Mennonite descent), and their two daughters. He and Sue cocoordinate indigenous work for Mennonite Central Committee (MCC) Canada; Harley was also codirector of the Anti-Racism Program of MCC United States from 2005 to 2008. Elaine interviewed Harley February 8, 2006.

Harley Eagle
Photo credit: Sue Eagle, used with permission

Shortly after Sue and I were married, we joined MCC to work with my relatives at Pine Ridge Reservation in South Dakota. Suddenly I was thrust into a situation where I was no longer the minority, but living on a reservation surrounded by my own people. Many on the reservation were living in unhealthy and unbalanced ways, but there were pockets of people who were very strong and knew who they were. These people helped to shape me.

During that time, I was given the opportunity to be trained in restorative justice. At first, I learned the dominant society's theory of restorative justice, but when I heard that its roots were in indigenous society, I was much more intrigued. As I was learning what it meant to be Dakota, I saw the correlation between our teachings and restorative justice theory. So during this period several things came together: I recognized my gifts in this work; I received counsel and direction from Sue and other women; I learned the Native teachings of my people; and I discovered a deep sense of belonging to and respect for a certain area of land.

I use the teachings of the medicine wheel to illuminate and practice restorative justice. I start in the spiritual quadrant, where we set the tone of the gathering, recognize power dynamics and bring people together, making sure it is a safe place for everyone. The emotional realm is where we hear the story of why we have come together, and everyone speaks their perspective, feelings, and pain surrounding the issue. We then move into the physical realm, where we start to examine the history and issues that brought us to this difficult place. Only after working through the previous quadrants can we move on to the intellectual realm where we make practical and good decisions together.

Harley does his work on antiracism and internalized oppression because of the questions and issues that are raised as one progresses through the medicine wheel. He is distressed by the fact that white restorative justice practitioners often do not pay attention to dynamics of social power, both in their diagnosis of a conflict and in their facilitation practice.

One of the primary goals of restorative justice facilitation is to avoid escalating harm. We who are mediators, circle facilitators, or trainers need to be aware of power and privilege in dominant society. When any of us walk into a room, the way we look, talk, or even our last name brings power dynamics. If we are not aware of this, or have not found a way to name and diffuse it, we are doing harm.

   The refusal of colleagues to examine or even acknowledge power dynamics has been one of my frustrations working with restorative justice groups. Restorative justice practitioners are usually well-intentioned people, with a strong desire to do something right and good for society. But if they do not recognize the difference between charity and true justice, they will violate people.

   In order to make significant changes in relationships that have been damaged by racism and internalized oppression, we must try different tactics, reflect on the results, and discuss it with others to see what is effective. Have relationships been damaged, strengthened, or deepened after a restorative justice process? But too many facilitators are not taking the time to reflect, because we are running ahead to do the next "cutting-edge" work. In particular, the dominant system tells men that we have to be charismatic leaders, and push to develop new programs. Often my white male colleagues do not take the time to slow down, look back, gather people and ask, "This is what I have done, can you help me reflect on it?"

Harley believes that because restorative justice processes are still based on white ways of doing things, the movement is missing many voices.

The voice of youth, for instance, is often excluded. At a recent meeting for our antiracism program, one of the committee members brought her eleven-year-old son. I invited him to join us in the meeting, telling him it was important he was there and that there was a place for him. He had a profound insight. Listening to us talk about who was not at the table, he responded, "Instead you should be worrying about whether you need a table or not." He is right: often the way we gather is exclusive. What we consider normal is alienating to others. We need to build more appropriate and inclusive processes.

Indigenous people have traditionally nurtured certain values in order to walk in a balanced way, such as humility and generosity. The dominant culture tells us we are supposed to be lifted up for the things that we have done; we are not supposed to be too generous with our time and wisdom. A lack of such humility and generosity are a consistent problem in the restorative justice movement.

The dominant society believes in the illusion of isolation; it convinces us that what we do has no effect on the larger world, let alone our neighbor. But before contact with Europeans, indigenous people had a good understanding of diversity and connection to land, place, and one another. We coexisted in a microcosm that was seeking to live in balance. Our society was not perfect; we knew we would make mistakes and that we needed to take care to practice ceremony and ritual. Our ceremonies taught us to walk in a way that was mindful of nature and how it operates. We are all interconnected, so what we do and say has direct bearing on our relatives around and beyond us.

Another concern is the way in which non-Native restorative justice practitioners try to appropriate Native practices or teachings into their own process, with no proper recognition, context, or respect.

It doesn't fit, because one teaching does not work in isolation. I am frustrated about this, but my responsibility is to help people learn to appreciate, not appropriate. I have spent considerable time talking with others who are disappointed with the white restorative justice movement, as well as with folks that do not understand why we are aggravated. I am now able to say, "What did we expect?" This movement arose from the dominant culture, and therefore is warped in the same ways. This realization helps me talk about the sickness of the system, rather than focus on individual, abusive behavior.

Harley acknowledges that he, too, has issues to work on, and that such work is integral to all of us who practice restorative justice.

My colleague and friend Ruth Yellowhawk and I provide trainings on racism, internalized oppression, and healing for Natives and non-Natives. We use books written by Native authors, so all of us focus on the teachings of Native people through the words of Native authors.

We provide tools and skill building for families to get together and participate in a circle process which allows for talking, listening, and exploring issues.

We believe that we, as facilitators, can't talk about this work unless we are doing it in our own lives and families. When I first started training I wasn't as focused on myself, but now I am committed to my own healing. It is the hardest work. The dominant society tells men that the most important work is changing the world, or the justice system or the institution. That is important, but if you are not doing your own healing work and if your family isn't along with you, the most authentic pieces are missing.

As I walk on this journey as a man, I have come to recognize and be wary of male privilege. I haven't been given all the privileges of powerful men, because I am not white or wealthy. But this society has taught me lies that are abusive towards women, the environment, and children, and we have learned to accept abusive relationships and behaviors as normal. This has led me to listen very carefully to the women in my life and to take direction from them. My work attempts to bring this to awareness, expose these lies, raise questions, and find possibilities for healing. If we men truly recognize that our behavior is often abusive, and has hurt us as well as others, we need to go back and figure out how to develop as true human beings, and rediscover how to be with one another and to listen and speak in respectful ways.

Traditionally we consider men to be "air creatures," and women as the "drumbeat" of Mother Earth. Our ways of thinking are different. Women and men need to have an understanding and trust of each other's gifts and roles, so we can work together. The dominant society tells men that women's talents and natural ways of being are inferior, and that we have no need to listen to them. I am learning to challenge my male colleagues and friends to listen to the women in their lives, rather than running to lead the movement, or to do something big and fantastic.

One of the ways we as men are stunted is that we were not taught to express ourselves or to trust our emotions. We are also taught to not trust women because they are emotional and express feelings; women are less important, so therefore feelings are less important. There is much work to be done in restorative justice circles to encourage men to express feelings.

Hopefully men will come to a greater understanding of power dynamics, and realize they too have been duped and hurt by this system. I do not think I will ever fully learn what it means to be a man, but hopefully my nephews will, if I can help change their worldview back to what is good for this earth.

Harley's experience with his wife, who is non-Native, gives him hope.

We Dakota have seven sacred teachings and ceremonies that are considered foundational. One of them is called the *hunka*, which means making a relative. Traditionally we would do this ceremony with strangers coming into our land who we knew shared our values. These new relatives became even closer to us than our blood relatives, and our mutual responsibilities were very important.

As a European Canadian, Sue has come to realize that she must learn to be a good guest on this land, and her thinking resonates profoundly with this ceremony. White and Native people could become relatives if we shared mutual respect, if we met in a way where Native people could say, "The same things are important to you as to us: the health of the children and of the land, and finding a way of living in balance, not greed." Then we could become relatives and walk together on this land.

Rarely in the voluminous recent literature on restorative justice—written largely by white theorists and practitioners like ourselves—is it clearly acknowledged that the contemporary movement is only discovering what has long been practiced among indigenous peoples throughout the world. Before European colonization, native people understood justice fundamentally in relational terms.[4] Personal (or tribal) offenses were seen as resulting either from ignorance or illness of the soul: one required teaching, the other, healing. Today, many tribes in Canada and the United States are rehabilitating traditional responses to crime and injustice, using sweat lodges, smudges, healing circles, and the medicine wheel to work toward restoration, accountability, and forgiveness. As non-Native teachers and practitioners of restorative justice, we believe it is important to recognize, honor, and learn from the older tradition of indigenous peoples and from contemporary interpreters like Harley Eagle.

In order to integrate Harley's concerns with the models presented in this chapter, we conclude with some practical reflections—drawn from Elaine's experience—about how to keep social power paramount in restorative justice facilitation. There are three stages of the process that must be

---

4. As does the Hebrew Bible and Jesus (see volume I, chapter 3). For recent books on indigenous justice, see McCaslin (2005); Ross (1996); Llewellyn, Ross, and Hoebel (2002); and Waziyatawin (2008). See also Chief Lawrence Hart's comments below (7A).

analyzed. The first stage is everything prior to the facilitation itself: the context, the offense, and the prosecution. It must be acknowledged that *any* victim-offender dialogue process has inherent power inequalities. On one hand, the offender has in some way exerted power over the victim, a gestalt that can continue well beyond the violation itself. On the other hand, insofar as a victim-offender reconciliation process occurs in the context of the criminal justice system, the offender is under the constraining and coercive power of a retributive, racist, and classist system, whereas the victim is free to come or go. This is why many restorative justice practitioners refer to their role in a victim-offender dialogue as "facilitation" rather than "mediation," since the latter term presupposes a conflict resolution process between relative social equals.[5]

Beyond these obvious ones, there are a myriad of other power issues related to the respective social locations of offender and victim, particularly regarding disparities between them. Broader contextual social analysis of the case is also needed in order to understand this particular offense relative to racial and economic patterns of crime and law enforcement playing out in this community.

The second stage is the dialogue itself, in which we can identify situational, relational, and institutional matrices of power dynamics. Facilitators are usually well trained in *situational* dynamics. This includes attention to such issues as the timing and location of the meeting(s); how the room is physically arranged so that all parties will feel as comfortable and nonthreatened as possible; even how the facilitator positions herself in relation to the victim, the offender, and their respective support persons.

There is a lot of room for improvement, however, when it comes to training facilitators in *relational* dynamics—the social factors that are at play within and between the participants. We can easily identify three:

- *Differences between persons in the room.* Some are obvious, such as language, age, and gender. Yet Elaine worked for years for a VORP in a city that was 50 percent Latino, and they only had a couple of Spanish speaking mediators! Are teens or women in the room getting adequate airtime and respect? Some differences are subtle but crucial, such as cultural protocols for expressing greetings or anger or remorse. Often participants are marginalized because differences are ignored or minimized, either out of ignorance or worse, because of unexamined patterns, such as the kind of male or white privilege Harley speaks about. The dialogue *process* is always a cross-cultural exercise requiring acute sensitivity to nonverbal scripts.

---

5. See above, 2B, nn. 7 and 8. See also Kritek (1994).

- *Disparities of power among participants (including the facilitator).* These include:
  - Educational background, including basic literacy.[6]
  - Access to networks of power (for example, the facilitator knows the referring judge) or association with networks considered "negative" (the offender is a gang member).
  - Race. While some 80 percent of the offenders (and 50 percent of the victims) Elaine has met in the past twenty years are people of color, 85 percent of the VORP mediators she has met are white, and often miss the racial dynamics.[7]
  - Economic status. This includes ability of parties involved to: hire counsel (or counselors!), miss work, travel to a VORP meeting, and so forth.
- *Different **vulnerabilities** of victim and offender.* The victim of an assault may be psychologically fragile, for example, blaming herself for what happened, while the offender may be feeling shamed by family members in the room who are angry at his behavior. Or each party might be feeling socioeconomic vulnerability: the offender in a car theft is in dangerous debt to local bookies, while the victim has lost his job because of an inability to get to work.

If these power dynamics remain invisible, they function like an elephant in the room. On the other hand, if they are allowed to surface in the storytelling, they can help to explain behavior, to discharge feelings, and to contribute to a more holistic resolution.

These are factors internal to the dialogue process, but there are also factors of *external institutional* power that exert influence on the process going on in the room. Were incentives or mandates used to get the offender to the table (e.g., threats of prosecution or promises of leniency)? Did the victim's pastor insist that she go to mediation because it is the "right" thing to do (which may mean she is there resentfully)? Are there legal issues or sanctions that constrain the facilitation? Who is covering the costs of

---

6. Elaine facilitated a case with a young man accused of threatening school staff. During the meeting, the boy's grandmother surprised everyone (including his teacher and the principal) by revealing that he was frustrated at school because he couldn't read! Grandma then proceeded to tell how both she and the boy's mother had also struggled with social marginalization due to illiteracy. That was the turning point of the dialogue and suggests how important social factors are in understanding the roots of a conflict.

7. Elaine cites an assault case involving a white and a black youth. Halfway through the dialogue, the facilitator noticed that the white boy's baseball cap had racial epithets written under the bill. The facilitator did not know how to handle this, and did nothing. Later, the black family contacted the VORP office, upset that their son had been revictimized by the same racial taunting that had led to the original assault.

training the facilitators and running the program—a church coalition or the probation department?—and how does that affect the dynamics of the process?

The third stage is after the dialogue process has concluded. As Harley Eagle asks, has the resolution contributed to some redistribution of power, or further polarization? Will the parties work with ongoing, wider community strategies that are addressing the power imbalances that have been identified in the dialogue process? As Nelson Johnson points out (below, 7B, ii), the long-term success of the community truth and reconciliation process in Greensboro will only be determined by structural changes in the educational, legal, and law enforcement systems—and that is an organizing task.[8]

These are some of the reasons why restorative justice facilitators need to map power dynamics and take inventory—before, during, and after the dialogue process. Social power *can* be discerned, though it is complex and variable according to context, and it is up to us to be diligent in our investigation. Training can better equip us in our work—but currently too few restorative justice trainings include cross-cultural, gender, and anti-racism work (it wasn't part of Elaine's education in the field, for example). And we need to develop strategies for how to handle race, class, or gender dynamics as they surface, so we are neither surprised nor unprepared during a dialogue.

Restorative justice practitioners are constantly navigating uneven, contested terrain in our efforts to resolve violations. We believe that the three tasks commended here in part 1—probing the roots of violence, tending the branches of the whole peacemaking tree, and testing the soil of each conflict to see how it is shaped by factors of social power—are all necessary if we are to be true ambassadors of reconciliation. We turn now to the testimonies of colleagues who are making this word flesh in some of the most difficult terrains in North America and beyond—because ultimately, the vision of restorative justice and peacemaking will gain traction not through theorizing but through practice.

---

8. Dugan (1996) similarly asserts the need for restorative justice practitioners not only to work at the "issue" and "relationship" levels of a conflict, but also to partner with those working at the "subsystem" and "systemic" levels.

Part Two

Contemporary Pioneers of Restorative Justice and Peacemaking

Having offered basic conceptual models and social analysis germane to the work of contemporary restorative justice and peacemaking, we now turn to the work of disciples whose practices embody and illustrate this theory. In our opinion, these mentors and friends are, like Harley Eagle, exemplary "ambassadors of reconciliation" in our historical moment, engaged in trying to heal and restrain the scourge of violence in our world, whether manifested as poverty, discrimination, war, or the death penalty.

Joe Avila, Marietta Jaeger Lane, Myrna Bethke, James Loney, Liz McAlister, Murphy Davis, Lawrence Hart, and Nelson Johnson hail from different denominational backgrounds and diverse geographical and generational contexts, and represent distinct modes of nonviolent engagement for justice and peace. Their witness incarnates the New Testament vision of restorative justice and peacemaking articulated in volume I of this project: Paul's call in 2 Corinthians 5-6 to work for truth and reconciliation; nonviolent direct action inspired by the Jesus of Mark 1-3; the restorative justice spirit of Matthew 18; and a defiance of dividing walls because of Christ's abolition of enmity as articulated in Ephesians.

We recognize that our choice to focus on individuals, rather than upon broader social movements, carries with it the danger of playing into three common misperceptions in our culture regarding such work:

- the tendency to overpersonalize or overdramatize efforts that are in fact the result of long-term, strategic engagement of many people and organizations over time, most of which is quite ordinary, often invisible and rarely measurable;
- the common assumption—nurtured in the media—that peace and justice work is all about solitary moral giants, rather than community initiatives amid complex cultural contexts and historical forces;

- the misperception that this work is primarily animated and sustained through individual conscience, rather than through relational networks, communal formation and disciplined collaboration.

We acknowledge these dangers and hope the reader will do the same, being particularly vigilant not to succumb to the temptation to think that the "heroic" lives of others exonerate us from response-ability. Still, our choice was deliberate, based on a conviction that for most North Americans, personal narrative tends to be more engaging than social and historical analysis alone. We believe that these stories are empowering and energizing in a culture paralyzed by a lack of political imagination.

4

VICTIMS AND OFFENDERS

From Violence to Healing

In forgiving, people are not being asked to forget. On the contrary, it is important to remember, so that we should not let such atrocities happen again. Forgiveness does not mean condoning what has been done. It means taking what happened seriously . . . , drawing out the sting in the memory that threatens to poison our entire existence.
—Desmond Tutu (1999: 271)

Forgiveness breaks the chain of causality because he who forgives you—out of love—takes upon himself the consequences of what you have done. Forgiveness, therefore, always entails a sacrifice.
—Dag Hammarskjold (1964: 173)

At the heart of Jesus' teaching on how a community should respond to violation in Matthew 18 is his double concern for the "least" (victims) and the "lost" (perpetrators). He understands that the only antidote to the spiral of violence (above, chapter 1) is a "seventy times seven" practice of restorative justice that exceeds "Lamech's curse" in its rigor and commitment (Matt 18:22; Gen 4:24).[1] The task of building an alternative culture of restoration in a society predicated on retribution, however, will take generations.

In 1974, in the small town of Elmira, Ontario, two young men went on a vandalism spree, damaging twenty-two different properties.[2] The offenders were assigned to a probation officer who was part of an informal

---

1. See our examination of these texts in volume I, chapter 3.
2. A description of this case, which led to the first VORP, can be found in Cayley (1998: 215-17).

study group that gathered to reflect on justice issues. In discussing the situation the idea emerged that in order to move toward healing, these young men should meet with their victims and pay them back for damages. This led to other, similar experiments, which eventually grew into the first Victim Offender Reconciliation Program (VORP).[3] VORP has subsequently become the backbone of the contemporary restorative justice movement.

VORP's main purpose is to bring victims, offenders, their families, and support people together in face-to-face meetings, in order to provide an opportunity for accountability, restitution, healing, and even forgiveness. The VORP process is led by trained facilitators, who meet first with both parties individually to prepare them to come together and talk with as much honesty and sincerity as possible. For some offenses, such as property crimes, only one preparatory meeting is needed. When the crime is violent, involving bodily injury or death, preparation may require many meetings over a number of years. In the face-to-face meetings, offenders hear, often for the first time, the consequences of their actions for the victim, victim's family and community, as well as for their own family. Victims, in turn, have their questions answered and their story vindicated, and are able to express their feelings directly to the person who caused them harm. When the offender is able to express remorse and make covenants around future behavior, healing for both offender and victim can occur.

In August 1989, Elaine came from Canada on Mennonite Voluntary Service to Fresno, California, to work with the local VORP. Her work with VORP became a deeper calling, and over the past twenty years she has worked as a restorative justice trainer and facilitator. She has met many extraordinary people, both victims and offenders, two of whom are profiled in this chapter. Each of these testimonies shows the power of restorative justice to transform even the worst-case scenario.

4A. Joe Avila of Prison Fellowship

It was in her role as a VORP facilitator that Elaine met Joe Avila, who she interviewed in Fresno on May 19, 2006. Joe killed Amy Wall in a drunk-driving accident on September 18, 1992. Joe was known in his community

---

3. There are many different victim-offender dialogue programs throughout North America and around the world. The term VORP was common during the early period when most programs were ministries of local churches. Now programs are also administered by probation departments, community mediation centers, and other organizations, and are variously referred to as Victim Offender Restitution Services, Victim Offender Mediation Program, Victim Offender Dialogue, and so forth (see Zehr, 1990).

Joe Avila

Photo credit: Prison Fellowship,
used with permission

as a good family man, married with two young daughters. He worked as a communications consultant for a national firm and was involved in his community and his daughters' schools. Amy was a high school student, the daughter of Rick and Linda Wall. She was a gifted leader in school and church, had many friends, and enjoyed cheerleading.

i. Walking the "Bridge of Sighs"

Immediately after the accident, Joe was held at Fresno County jail. A friend of his called the VORP office asking if someone would talk with Joe. Two weeks later, Elaine and a colleague went to the jail and spoke with Joe. His slumped body and ashen face showed his devastation.

> In those first days I was contemplating suicide, convinced that this was the end. Not only had I made a shambles of my relationship with my wife, my children, my family, and my community, I had killed someone. Everything was wrong. A chaplain came to visit me and talked about sin and forgiveness, and told me that Jesus Christ died on the cross even for what I did five days ago. It was profound for me to hear him say that. The chaplain gave me a Gideon's small bible, which I have to this day. I began reading the Gospels and found stories about restoration and forgiveness. A couple of weeks later you came to see me.

Joe's trial was highly publicized. He had six prior drunk driving charges, and the prosecutor was looking to make an example of him. The court-room was packed with Amy's family and friends, and also Joe's supporters. Joe's attorney began by arguing that Joe was not responsible for Amy's death, because the tree that her car hit after being struck by Joe's vehicle was planted too close to the freeway.

> The strategy of my attorney was to prolong, postpone, and detain my proceedings until the fervor around my case would go away. There was enough judicial process to go on and on. That is the point: to wear the process down in order to get the smallest sentence. But this strategy continually victimizes the plaintiffs. Everyday the courtroom was filled with Amy's friends, family, and schoolmates. I

reached a point where I felt enough was enough. But I knew that if I changed my plea, I was going to prison for a long time.

At the beginning of my trial, I was grasping at straws. But over the months, I matured and learned more of God's saving grace and mercy. Eventually I was interested in changing my life and being at peace with who I had become. From you I learned about a restorative model, and began to accept responsibility for my life and choices.

In March 1993, just before Easter, my wife, Mary, and I decided to change my plea to guilty. I did not want to drag the victims through any more pain. My attorney tried to dissuade us, saying I would get the maximum sentence, and that there were many tactics yet to try. But Mary and I were clear.

The legal system makes it difficult for offenders to take responsibility for their crimes. After Joe's arrest the Avilas received numerous solicitations from trial lawyers promising to get him "off." The conventional wisdom is to avoid a guilty plea because of the retributive consequences that follow. This often leads to plea bargaining or attempts to get off on legal technicalities. This illustrates one of the central problems in the criminal justice system (CJS) that restorative justice seeks to address. The CJS asks three basic questions when a crime is committed:

1. What law was broken?
2. Who did it?
3. What punishment do they deserve?

Crimes are considered offenses against the state, and the offender is accountable to the law, not the victim. But the time Joe eventually served in jail as punishment did little to ease the pain of Amy's family.

Restorative justice, in contrast, understands violation to be social and relational, asking three very different questions (Zehr, 2002: 21):

1. Who was harmed by the crime?
2. What are their needs?
3. Whose obligation is it to meet those needs?

Victim-offender dialogue attempts to help offenders acknowledge how they have hurt victims and their community, and to figure out—preferably with help from victims—how to repair the damage and ensure that further violations will not occur. Through this process, some of the victims' needs are met, and the offender is held accountable to the social relationship that has been violated.

It was with this new understanding that Joe decided to abandon efforts at legal maneuvering designed to minimize his responsibility and lighten his sentence. Instead, he chose to plead guilty in order to spare his victim's family the further pain of an adversarial trial. The following weeks were taxing. Mary received a copy of probationary reports stating that Joe would get the maximum sentence of twelve years. The reports included many letters from the victims and the community pushing for the maximum sentence.

> Mary had also collected letters on my behalf, but we chose not to use them. All of the letters from Amy's community were asking the judge to lock me up and throw away the key.

The day of sentencing is grueling for everyone. People in the courtroom must relive the accident over and over, as prosecutor and defense attorney each plead their case. At the end of the proceedings, after everything is decided, victims are allowed to address the offender directly, but at that point, most offenders are saturated.

> I believe that any offender should be willing to hear from their victims. But at the end of the proceedings, I was so numb I was oblivious to most of their comments. I remember some of what people said, but certainly not all of it. And that is most offenders' experience.

Joe was given the maximum sentence of twelve years and was immediately remanded into custody.

Reflecting on the very first moments after sentencing, Joe recalled a prison he had recently visited.

> Mary and I went to Doge's Palace in Venice. The tour guide showed us the dungeons and prisons. Then we walked the "Bridge of Sighs" which was the bridge a prisoner walked just after learning his sentence. As he walks he begins to realize the consequences. His sighs are his fears. After I was sentenced, I walked, by myself, down a very long, underground tunnel. All prisoners in Fresno County Jail walk that tunnel. It is a quarter-mile long with no windows. That is where we reflect on what we have done and what is in store for us. I never want to be down there again. That was my "bridge of sighs."

In many ways the Avila family was fortunate, because Joe was sentenced to California Men's Colony, only 150 miles from their home in Fresno. Mary and their daughters, Elizabeth and Grace, were able to visit Joe about once a month.

Joe was allowed to make a brief phone call every other day, which is considered to be a privilege while incarcerated.

> Prison was not a good experience, but it was all I had for many years, so I tried to make the best of it. God gave me favor in prison, but there were some situations I would never want to repeat. Mary and I decided that our phone calls would be mostly superficial, a time for me to say hello to the girls and to pray together, but we would not talk about anything serious. We made the decision that if something was critical (like when Mary lost her job) we would talk about it only when Mary could be with me in person.
>
> In prison you don't have control of the phone and you only have a few minutes to talk even if you just got difficult news. There are more suicides in prison because of five minute phone calls than anything else. So Mary and I were very deliberate in that decision. We called to encourage each other and share whatever the good news was—such as Grace scoring a goal in a game. The more serious discussions we had through letters or a visit. I was also given work detail that allowed me to minister at the prison hospital, where people were dying of AIDS and cancer. God prepared me to do that and put me in a position of trust. I prayed often with dying men.

Once incarcerated, Joe devoted himself to self-examination. He invited us a number of times to speak to other inmates about forgiveness and reconciliation. We met with men who were lifers, who had killed someone and had no chance of ever getting out. We listened to their anguish-filled stories, and then prayed together. Joe even organized a Weekend of Reconciliation with God, family, friends, and community. Joe was committed to the hard work of personal transformation and encouraged others in prison to do the same. During this time we also started meeting regularly with Mary to support her while Joe was incarcerated.

ii. To Make Amends

When Joe spoke of the day he was released, he became very emotional.

> Elizabeth was a senior in high school. When I arrived home she brought all of her friends over to meet me, introducing me with pride: "This is my dad!" Her friends all gave me a hug. It was an extraordinary witness to me; when we do something wrong but have worked to make things right, we do not have to hide. Both Elizabeth and Grace told their friends what I had done and that I was

in prison; everyone at their school knew, but no one used it against them. I was out in time for Elizabeth's high school graduation and prom, but I missed many important years. Elizabeth has given her testimony all over the country, and she is not embarrassed to say, "My dad was not there for my first date." She does not say it out of a hurt place anymore; she has made peace with me being gone all of those years.

While Joe was in prison, Mary was embraced by people from Prison Fellowship, an organization that partners with local churches across the country to minister to prisoners, ex-prisoners, and their families.[4] The Fellowship helped Mary learn how to cope and how to support Joe and their daughters, and explained the rules and regulations of prison visitation. Joe was released from prison on January 6, 1999, after serving seven years. The next day, he met with leaders of Prison Fellowship and began to volunteer for them. One year from his release date, Joe was hired to work with the organization, and currently Joe is the executive director of their western region.

Joe has organized a program called Celebrate Recovery, an explicitly Christian version of the twelve-step program.

Celebrate Recovery was so successful on the outside that we decided to bring it into prison. When prisoners are released we try to get them involved in churches, but it is rarely successful because prisoners are intimidated and afraid, and the church doesn't really want them. When people in recovery get out of prison, they cannot find support. People in recovery are drawn to each other, we know who we are. We are a bunch of misfits trying to deal with our bad habits and addictions. We recognize that we drink too much, and are powerless over it. Celebrate Recovery is now in fifteen prisons and we continue to grow. Inmates see Celebrate Recovery as a safe place in prison and when they get out, they can immediately bridge into another Celebrate Recovery group, which they recognize as a safe environment on the outside.

Joe is also committed to preventing the violence of drunk driving, and works with the Fresno Police Department as an educator. This has encouraged his youngest daughter, Grace, to take up the same cause. Grace was six years old when Joe was sent to prison. Having grown up heavily impacted by the consequences of drinking and driving, she wanted to help

---

4. Information on Prison Fellowship can be found at www.prisonfellowship.org/. For a narrative of their work with children of prisoners see Colson and Earley (2003).

prevent such tragedies. She developed an idea her father had for reaching out to people arrested for driving under the influence.

> Right after I offended, Mary received thirty to fifty letters from different attorneys with the same message: "Everybody drives drunk; if you pay us these fees, we will get you off." They were soliciting business at a time when I was most vulnerable. When someone is arrested, cited, or escorted home for being intoxicated, they wake up the next morning hung-over, depressed, angry, and weary. At that time they are perhaps most remorseful and their hearts may be open to hearing something different. We thought if attorneys can use this moment, so can we.
>
> Grace developed a brochure to build awareness of the inevitable consequences of driving while under the influence. It provides a list of resources for alcoholism and drug addiction, and the story of what happened in her life. We had thousands of these printed. All patrolmen in Fresno now have brochures in their cars and motorcycles, so when someone is stopped for driving under the influence, they are given one. I am sure this brochure has saved a life already.

Three students at Grace's school were involved in a drunk driving accident. The driver lost control of the vehicle, and though he walked away, the other two were killed. Imagining the horror of his morning after, Joe immediately went to talk with him. "Grace's brochure is titled TMA, which stands for 'The Morning After,'" says Joe. "To us, however, it also means 'To Make Amends,' and we hope it leads to that."

Shortly after the accident Joe expressed a desire to meet with Amy Wall's family. We contacted them through their pastor but they were not interested in talking with us. After Joe was released from prison he did meet with the Walls' pastor, but the family still chose not to meet. For Joe, to meet his victims would have been an extraordinary gift, but it seemed that this was not going to happen.

> I made my peace, processed my grief and disappointment. I would continue to advocate against drunk driving, which was my work to do now. Even though I would not get to meet the Walls, I was doing the work God put before me.

Since his release from prison, Joe has given hundreds of talks to prisoners, churches, communities, and youth at risk. The traffic division of the Fresno Police Department retains him to tell his story to help stop the senseless deaths caused by drunk driving.

It is grueling work to revisit the horror, pain, and responsibility of taking someone's life. But Joe's willingness to repeat his story led to a great gift.

It never gets any easier to tell my story, but God provides me energy. One evening around Thanksgiving 2005, Police Chief Dyer was asked to speak on KMJ radio. The station was doing a preventative program on drinking and driving during the holidays, and Chief Dyer invited me to speak. Rick Wall, the father of Amy, was driving on the highway and the only station that had reception was KMJ. He was going to turn it off, but then heard that I was going to be on. He called his son Derek immediately and they both listened to the entire program.

Two days later, Amy's brother Derek, contacted the VORP office and asked to meet with Joe.

In that moment, I was completely blindsided. What I thought I had come to peace with was suddenly open and raw again. But clearly I would meet with Derek.

When bringing victims and offenders together, facilitators ask them to invite support people and to think through the many details of meeting under such difficult circumstances. Derek chose to bring his pastor. Joe and Mary came together.

All the details around the meeting were set – who would be there, what time we would each arrive, how we would greet each other, where we would sit, who would speak first. The facilitator opened the meeting with prayer and general rules, one of which was to paraphrase each other. The paraphrasing was very awkward and finally Derek asked, "Can we just talk?" And so we did. We talked about the past. Derek told me about growing up with his sister and how much he loved her. On the night she was killed, he thought of me as an animal. I talked about growing up and the acute alcoholism I went through, offering no excuses, but accepting responsibility for my actions. We talked for quite some time with much pain and tears.

Near the end of the meeting, I again offered my apologies and Derek accepted them. Then he reached in his pocket and brought out a key chain. During the trial, the court room was full of high school students carrying key chains with a picture of Amy on one side and these words on the other, "Someone drank and drove, and Amy died." Derek had recently added the words, ". . . so others might live." As Derek gave me the key chain, he said, "Whether we like it or not, now we are together. And it is not just my problem anymore, it is our problem. Hopefully, down the road, you and I will be working together."

It was an absolute miracle and an incredibly emotional event. In the book of Philemon, when Paul intercedes for Onesimus he writes, "I want you to restore him, not as a slave but as a brother in Christ." That is what is happening between Derek and me. Through restorative justice something that absolutely defies nature happens. Who in their right mind would want to forgive someone who killed their sibling?

Shortly after Joe was informed that Amy's father, Rick, also wanted to meet. They met on February 8, 2006.

Rick came in with a legal pad and I could tell he was "prayed up." He had three things he wanted to talk about: the past, the present, and the future. He began by talking about Amy—what a wonderful person she was, about the night she was killed, how it felt to lose a daughter. Rick then described how he goes to the cemetery twice a year, on Amy's birthday and on the day she was killed.

He told me that I had paid my debt to society by serving time, and by society's standards I wasn't required to do anything else. He acknowledged that I was in prison for a long time, and after my release I could have become invisible, but that I had chosen not to. He was aware of the work that I was doing. Then he told me, "I want you to know that I forgive you. If you are going to continue this work, I give you permission to use my daughter's name and picture in your cause." This was an amazing gift to me, since prior to this I had never used Amy's name when I told my story.

The meeting with Rick was short. He was talking with the man who killed his daughter, and had the opportunity to say anything he wanted to say, yet he chose to make it brief. I believe he did that for me. He did not want to see me go through an anguish-filled night.

Joe and Mary had hoped also for a meeting with Amy's mother, Linda, but did not know if it would happen. Four months after our interview, Elaine received this letter from Joe:

I would like to take this opportunity to thank you for your prayers these past few days. Last Thursday night I viewed a three-hour video of Amy Wall's life at the request of Linda Wall. The video was very painful to watch, yet I got to know Amy and how precious she was to her family, friends and community. God also revealed to me that since I had been telling my story to thousands of people, this video would help me tell it better. I will always be grateful for the privilege of getting to know Amy in this way.

The next night Mary and I met with Linda, along with her uncle and our mediators. Our meeting lasted two and one half hours, mostly exchanged statements between Linda and me. It was evident that her pain and anger was just as intense as fourteen years ago. I am praying that perhaps, by releasing and directing this pain and anger towards me, she will begin to heal. I am thankful I had the opportunity to tell her how sorry I am for taking her daughter's life and for all the pain I had caused her, her family and community. That night was a fire I would not like to walk through again. But I will; we made some agreements that are very positive and may lead to another meeting in the future. Maybe some healing will occur by then.

Linda has also given me permission to use Amy's picture and name in the materials I have produced to educate young people on the dangers of driving while under the influence of alcohol or drugs. She has also requested a recording of some of my appearances and speaking engagements. I hope these will give some sense of what I am doing to honor her daughter's life.

Until the day when I first met Derek, I had never looked at Amy's picture. When Derek gave me her picture, I could look at it with peace. It is now in our office at Prison Fellowship and I see it every day.

All of the persons we have met in our work who have committed serious crimes, then courageously devoted their lives to making things right, have wrestled with the multiple layers of forgiveness. So too Joe:

Forgiveness was a struggle for me for a long time. I knew that I had to forgive myself at some point, but I first had to learn what unconditional forgiveness was. Forgiveness is not about relentlessly reminding myself of the wrong I did. First of all God forgave me, then Mary and my children and extended family and friends. I believe that those in the Fresno community who know who I am have forgiven me, because they know what I did and what I now do. I was the last one to forgive myself.

Forgiveness has nothing to do with the time I served. I often felt guilty laughing or having a good time, and I had to work to overcome that. And I wrestle with guilt about the men I served time with, who are still in prison for the same offense as I. Tears well up when I feel I do not deserve all the goodness that God has given me. A lot of times we are not deserving of God's grace, but we have to learn to accept it and celebrate it as a gift. When I finally realized that I am indeed forgiven, I began to move on. And it was an unbelievable gift that Rick and Derek extended their forgiveness to me.

It has been a journey full of hard work. God tests my endurance at the most inconvenient times. I detest public speaking, preferring to remain in the background. But I am committed to telling my story, because so many people are desperate for a way out. That is why I tell my story whenever asked, even when I don't want to. And I always walk away with a blessing. All the work I do is to honor Amy's life.[5]

4B. Marietta Jaeger Lane
of Murder Victim Families for Human Rights

Marietta Jaeger Lane, after planting a Mountain Ash at site where Susie was kidnapped in Montana, October 2008.

Photo credit: Journey of Hope, used with permission

---

5. On February 13, 2009, Joe and Derek spoke together at Fresno Pacific University; Amy's parents were both in attendance. A DVD of their presentation is available at http://peace.fresno.edu/rjp/.

The same year that the first experiment with VORP was being launched in Ontario, a story of personal tragedy and agonizing grief was unfolding in Montana. Yet the same spirit that was moving those working with juvenile offenders would inspire Marietta Jaeger to become a pioneer in restorative justice as she faced the worst-case scenario: the murder of her seven-year-old daughter, Susie.[6]

In the early hours of June 25, 1974, Marietta received a phone call. It was the one-year anniversary of Susie's abduction. When Marietta had gone to bed earlier that night, her prayer was that somehow God would mark this day by allowing something pertinent to happen in the investigation. Marietta did not recognize the voice on the phone, but she was holding on to a thin thread of hope that Susie was still alive. She exulted as she realized she was speaking to the man who had kidnapped her daughter.

A year earlier, Marietta, her husband, and their five children had packed up their car in Michigan, offered a prayer for traveling mercies, and set off for a family camping trip. They arrived at Missouri River Headwaters Monument campground, just outside of Three Forks, Montana. Marietta and the kids explored the banks of the mighty river and the vast valley surrounded by majestic snow-tipped mountains. Susie, the youngest child, was high spirited, full of laughter and adventure. She was tall and athletic, and her brown, wavy hair spun in the air as she did cartwheels in rapid succession.

On Sunday, the Jaeger family went to a nearby church for Mass. In the middle of that night—despite outside lights and people and dogs sleeping under the stars—a young man named David was able to creep up to the Jaeger tent, cut a hole in the side, and stealthily pull Susie out. No one woke up. The dogs did not bark. At 5 A.M., one of Susie's siblings was awakened by a cold breeze and immediately noticed that Susie, who had been sleeping right beside her, was gone.

i. I Gave God Permission to Change My Heart

The Jaeger family immediately began their search while it was still dark. The FBI, sheriff's department, and many concerned local residents came to help look for Susie. The Jaeger family waited at the campsite for five weeks with no sign of Susie before finally returning to their home in Michigan. The FBI continued to investigate the case, but had no leads or clues. The day before the anniversary of Susie's disappearance, Marietta

---

6. Marietta's books in our bibliography are listed under Jaeger; she has since remarried, and goes by Jaeger Lane.

was interviewed by the Associated Press in Montana, expressing concern for the kidnapper. She stated she wanted to speak with the person who had taken her child, although after the elapse of a whole year, she feared that conversation was most unlikely.

In the middle of the night, one year exactly to the minute of Susie's abduction, Marietta received the call. "You wanted to talk to me? Here I am. But I am the one who is in control," David taunted. However, Marietta disarmed him by saying she had been praying for him and asked what she could do to help him. The young man began to cry, and continued to talk with Marietta for over an hour, revealing enough information for the FBI to identify him.

Three months later the FBI had built a case against David, a probable schizophrenic, who initially denied his guilt, and arrested him. Marietta told the investigators and prosecutors that she did not want the death penalty, and she met with David several times, expressing concern for him. When he finally confessed, Marietta learned the painful details of what had happened to Susie. She had been murdered two weeks after her abduction; David also confessed to three other local murders. Shortly thereafter, he hanged himself. In October 1974, sixteen months after Susie had disappeared, Marietta and her husband traveled back to Montana to give Susie a proper burial.[7]

I grew up in a house where we were never allowed to be angry. I was told that to be angry was a sin and that I would lose favor with God. As a result I was very adept at repressing my anger. It took two weeks of sitting at the campground picnic table waiting for any news of Susie for my rage to roil up through the many inhibitions I had placed on it. When I finally allowed myself to get in touch with my anger, I envisioned over and over what I could do if the FBI caught the kidnapper and said, "OK, Marietta have at him." I knew that I could kill the kidnapper with my bare hands and a smile on my face. Even before I knew what he had done to Susie, I could have killed him for the terror he put her through, for taking her away from us and the effect it had on my entire family.

However, after a major midnight wrestling match with God in which I tried to justify my "right" to rage and revenge, I "surrendered." Because I believe in a God who never violates our freedom or free will, I gave God permission to change my heart. I promised

---

7. Elaine interviewed Marietta in February 2006. Marietta has written several detailed accounts of her story: Jaeger (1983) and later, chapters in Enright and North (1998: 9-14) and Judah and Bryant (2004: 159ff.). See also the accounts of King (2003) and Barnett (1999).

to cooperate with God in whatever God could do to move my heart from fury to forgiveness.

There was a time in the beginning where I felt that if I forgave the kidnapper, I would be unfaithful to Susie. I also struggled with a belief common to victims of violence—that if I could stay angry and get revenge, I was in control.

I was catapulted into a very intense, spiritual journey, and spent many hours in prayer and reading scripture. God spoke to me frequently. It was a long, gradual process but, during that year, I came to realize three things:

- In staying full of rage I was in fact handing my power over to the kidnapper, allowing his actions to change my value system and lead me away from the direction I wanted my life to go.
- In God's eyes the kidnapper was just as precious as my little girl.
- And if I wanted to live my Catholic faith with integrity, I was called to forgive and pray for my enemies. I realized that I needed to forgive the kidnapper for the sake of myself and everyone who touched my life.

We lived for fifteen months with no word of what happened to Susie. During that time I believed that Susie was still alive because the kidnapper was calling sheriff deputies and FBI offices identifying Susie by an unpublished birth defect, saying he wanted to exchange her for ransom. I needed to be loyal to Susie, so no matter what it looked like and until I had tangible proof to the contrary, I made a deliberate, conscious decision to believe she was alive.

As the months went by with no word about Susie, I also prayed to know what God's idea of justice was. I came to understand that if Jesus is the word of God made flesh, then Jesus is the *justice* of God made flesh. As I looked at the life of Jesus in scripture I did not see someone who came to hurt, punish, or put us to death. Jesus came to heal and help us, to rehabilitate and reconcile us, to restore to us the life that was lost by "original sin." God's idea of justice is restoration, not punishment.

In wrestling with God my life was transformed, and by the time of the first anniversary call, the miracle of forgiveness had been accomplished in my heart. That miracle was not diminished even when I had to learn of and grieve all the horrible things that happened to Susie before and after her death. God does good work!

Part of my grief is that after the kidnapper was arrested and made his confession, he took his life. I had truly hoped he would be restored. But my hope was probably not realistic, because he was a very sick young man. He had killed a number of children and had never been discovered except by the phone call he made to me. My prayer for the kidnapper was that he too could have been healed. I am very grateful that God was so persistent in calling me to the faith that I want to live my life by.

Only a few months after Susie was buried, a local church contacted Marietta, asking her to speak to their women's group about how her faith sustained her through the ordeal. It had not occurred to Marietta that anyone would be interested in her experience, however extraordinary it was. She expected and intended to resume living as she had—as wife, mother, and homemaker. The invitation caught her completely by surprise.

> Could it be that God wants to do more with my faith journey than just teach me about the value of forgiveness? Could it be that God wants to use my story to help others? "But," I thought, "I am just a country bumpkin, a high school graduate with no training, skill, or experience in public speaking. What could I say that would be of value to anyone else?"

Marietta was hesitant about the invitation, and prayed about whether or not to accept it. Finally she decided that because it was a small gathering of church women on a Tuesday afternoon, she could do it.

Marietta determined that if God's hand was guiding this, she would know. But it was difficult and nerve-racking nonetheless.

> Remarkably, I got through that first presentation. After all, it was my life that I was speaking about, not a theological treatise I had memorized. Two of those present approached me afterward asking if I would come and speak at their churches. Those presentations led to more invitations and soon, without any design or desire on my part, a speaking ministry had evolved. As it grew, I began to see very clearly God's hand orchestrating these events. Reports came back from people who, after hearing my story, were compelled to forgive the people who had hurt and victimized them. People described marvelous stories of reconciliations, freedom from long-held hostilities and even physical healing.
>
> I began to see that God was using my story as a "contemporary parable" to speak to people bound in un-forgiveness. I began to understand that, though Susie's suffering and death was never God's perfect will, God was redeeming her death by making it a gift of life for others, just as Jesus' death on the cross is a gift of life for Chris-

tians. When I began to see what God was doing, I was able to fully assent to this ministry and call.

As a result of her speaking ministry, Marietta was exposed to people from the Catholic Worker community in Detroit, and occasionally she co-led retreats with them.[8]

> Through my interactions with the Catholic Worker I began to make the connection between my personal stance toward the man who had taken Susie's life and our nation's stance toward its enemies. I would never have been complicit in my little girl's death; how could I be silent about the violence and death my government's policies and practices were committing, in my name and with my tax dollars?

In 1983, after Marietta's husband died and her children had grown, she felt free to make changes in her lifestyle. She moved into inner-city Detroit and became part of the Catholic Worker Peace Community, participating often in retreats, discussions, prayer vigils, and demonstrations that included civil disobedience. Also during this time, to ensure that she was not contributing to the military budget, Marietta chose to live below a taxable income.[9]

> This provided an excellent opportunity to be in solidarity with the people in my neighborhood, living with the poor. After much persuasion, I was finally able to convince an elderly and extremely eccentric homeless woman to trust me enough to sleep in my tiny apartment, rather than on the streets, in the cold. But she would only come and stay with me during the winter months. Although I provided her with food and a bed for three years, I was convicted about how far I truly was from the generous and gracious hospitality of God.

Marietta has traveled all over the world and has testified before the United Nations Commission on Human Rights. Her primary work is to help people understand forgiveness and, in particular, to invite Christians to practice the difficult scriptural exhortation to love our enemies.

---

8. For information about the contemporary Catholic Worker movement see www .catholicworker.org. James Loney (below, 5B) is a member of this movement, and both Elizabeth McAlister and Murphy Davis claim the Catholic Worker tradition as well (chapter 6).

9. For information on war tax resistance as a strategy of conscience, see www.nwtrcc .org.

A common misconception about forgiveness is the familiar phrase to "forgive and forget." I will never forget what happened to Susie and our family. But it is precisely because I can't forget that I need to find a healthy, holy way to live with our violent loss. I will not stay chained to a past event, because no matter what I do, I can never change what happened to Susie and our family.

As Christians we are called to love our enemies, but most people simply dismiss this commandment. We associate the word "love" with warm fuzzies, and claim we could never feel that way towards the person who violated us. But what I came to understand is that the love of enemies God calls us to is a love that desires God's best for that person and a willingness to help them if we can.

In order to work toward loving our enemies, Marietta believes we must understand the spiral of violence (chapter 1) that so many offenders and victims in the criminal justice system are caught in:

I encourage victims to do as much as they can to understand the background of the offender. Generally speaking, violent offenders have been victimized themselves and have not known anything other then verbal, sexual, or physical abuse all their life. Knowing the offender's background does not condone anything they have done, but it can help facilitate a more compassionate mind-set among some victims. We can begin to understand why the offender became that kind of person and responded the way they did.

Every time we pray the Lord's Prayer we are making a covenant with God: "God forgive me my sins the way I forgive those who have sinned against me." I try to encourage people by admitting that on my own I could not rise to this prayer. I wanted to kill the person who kidnapped Susie. But God knows we are vulnerable and hurting, and loves us too much to give us principles to live by only to leave us helpless to do so. The power of the Holy Spirit is available to us so we can be the people that God calls us to be and do the things that faith requires us to do.

ii. We Will Not Create Another Victim

The emphasis of Marietta's early speaking engagements was on fury and forgiveness, but she also spoke about her opposition to the death penalty whenever she told Susie's story. While she was codirector of a local faith-oriented human rights organization, political forces began to push to introduce the death penalty in Michigan after a particularly brutal murder in Detroit.[10] Her organization decided to educate mainline denominations about the inefficacy, racial discrimination, public costs, and immorality of capital punishment. In her presentations, Marietta began emphasizing her position against the death penalty as the mother of a murder victim.

> We victims degrade and dehumanize ourselves by the practice of killing to appease our pain, and we put ourselves in the same mind-set as the murderer. The death penalty communicates to society that killing is an appropriate means for solving our problems. And because the death penalty is government sanctioned, there is an air of authority around it, as though it must be moral. But we have had all sorts of immoral legislation, such as slavery. As people become educated and hold government practices and policies to account before their values and principles, slowly but surely laws are changed. Politicians will go where the votes are. I feel God is calling me to specifically speak to the Christian community because so many of them are absolutely opposed to abortion but see capital punishment as proper.

As before, Marietta received more invitations to speak and began meeting other people whose loved ones were murder victims.

> Though every one of us who have had a loved one murdered would give everything not to be in this position, we find that we are a very credible and persuasive voice against the death penalty. We recognized our need for an organization that would pull us all together and provide a forum for our position. So in the early 1990s, I became a founding board member of Murder Victims' Families for Reconciliation (MVFR).

In June 1993, death penalty abolitionist organizers in Indiana invited members of MVFR to speak throughout the state.[11] Marietta participated in the two-week tour, addressing a variety of forums and speaking to the press. MVFR was invited to do a similar tour the following year in Georgia and California.

In 1997, to further focus the work of resistance to the death penalty, Marietta cofounded another organization: Journey of Hope—From Vio-

---

10. In 1847, when Michigan became a state, the very first act of the legislature was to abolish capital punishment, making it the first English-speaking territory in the world to do so. In 1963 the abolition of the death penalty was inscribed in the state constitution. A 2004 effort to introduce the death penalty in Michigan was defeated in the state legislature.

11. Bill Pelke was among them. Bill's grandmother was murdered by a fifteen-year-old girl who, after being convicted, was sent to death row.

lence to Healing. It has been on the forefront of the abolitionist movement since its inception.

> At least once a year, we do a two-week speaking tour through a state that executes people. We address every venue that is open to a discussion of our perspective on the death penalty: universities, high schools, church services, television or radio talk shows, media interviews, public debates, marches, and rallies. We have a few people who can speak about statistics and government legislation. But most of our speakers are people like me who share our personal stories of violence, and how and why we came to oppose the death penalty.
>
> Well-meaning people who recognize the fallibility, inefficacy, and financial waste of the death penalty will say, "But we need it as a matter of justice for the victim's family." We can say, like no one else can, that retaliatory executions cannot compensate us for what we have lost, or restore our loved ones to our arms. In fact, we insult the inestimable value of our loved ones' memories by becoming that which we abhor—people who kill people. We have to aspire to a higher moral principle that is more befitting the goodness and innocence of our loved ones' lives, a principle that claims all life is sacred and worthy of preservation. We will not resort to another killing of a chained, defenseless person, creating yet another victim and another grieving family.

In 2004, Marietta cofounded Murder Victims' Families for Human Rights (MVFHR), an international nongovernmental organization of family members of victims of criminal murder, terrorist killings, state executions, extrajudicial assassinations, and "disappearances." Their primary work is to oppose the death penalty from a human-rights perspective. Marietta regularly participates in actions against the death penalty and U.S. foreign policy (including the current war), and was arrested in January 2006 for blocking the steps of the Supreme Court during an anti–death penalty demonstration.

> I prefer to call the civil disobedience that I am involved in an act of "moral" or "divine" obedience. Principles that are operative in my personal life as I try to live out my faith with integrity are also pertinent on a larger scale. If I have to forgive the kidnapper and murderer of my little girl, then it is not right for me to kill another person or bomb an enemy nation. In my work I talk about the entire spectrum of violence, offering people a different understanding of forgiveness that counters the ways of the world and the Powers and Principalities that hold sway in our spirits.

Through these years of advocacy, Marietta has continued to work with victims of violence, encouraging them to find healing and wholeness. She is critical of a criminal justice system whose focus on the death penalty does not bring closure or healing to victims of violence. She calls on churches to offer an alternative and to be more active in their ministry to victims.

Many churches have prison ministries, but I don't know of one church that has a victim ministry. Most often, victim families become isolated. People do not want to intrude on victims' privacy, fearing that a visit might remind them of something they have been trying to forget. There is also a psychological phenomenon that is unconscious that says, "If I keep my distance, this terrible violence won't happen to me." But victim families need to be held, loved, prayed for, and listened to. They need to continually process their rage, loss, and grief so it won't fester. The Christian community that upholds the value of life and forgiveness needs to be present so that when the victims have processed most of their pain, they hear that the next, best move is to give God permission to change their hearts.

We need time and space to heal. If we break our leg we are not up and running the next day; bones take time to heal. We need even more healing when our hearts are broken. It is hard to be in the presence of someone who is suffering and be unable to do anything to change it. It is uncomfortable, and most people avoid it. Yet, what the victim family really needs is someone to listen to their story again and again, people who love us enough to have the patience to sit with us and help us move along.

In all the years that I have been working with murder victim family members, I see that however they feel—and initially it is a normal, valid human response to be filled with rage—to retain that vindictive mind-set only makes us unhappy, unhealthy, embittered people. It is tragic because victims feel so justified calling for the death penalty, while often the prosecutor pushes just to get another notch in his belt. Many prosecutors hold the death penalty out as a means of healing and closure for these people. Victims are vulnerable and disconsolate in their grief and rage, and so they buy into that lie. And because the church is often not present, victims are easy prey for prosecutors. They are then revictimized through the appeals process, having their wounds ripped open again. I cannot tell victims how to feel. What I try to do is share my story with them and hope that they will hear some truth in it for themselves.

On the twenty-fifth anniversary of Susie's abduction Marietta made a solo pilgrimage back to Montana where her daughter is buried. She had just completed a busy schedule of speaking and traveling, and was very tired.

I decided I would drive from Detroit to Montana by myself. I would have plenty of uninterrupted time to pray, meditate, and listen to books on tape. I would spend the twenty-fifth anniversary day in Montana and then drive back home again. I began that day by going to the little church in the town of Three Forks where we had worshipped together as a family the Sunday morning before Susie was taken. It seemed a good place to start my pilgrimage. As I walked into the church, I prayed, "God, twenty-five years ago you surprised me with grief and tragedy. How about today, for an anniversary present, you surprise me with joy?" It was a spontaneous prayer, I had no agenda. I walked into the church and met my future husband.

Marietta married Bob Lane and left innercity Detroit for his sprawling ranch in Three Forks. She remains an active member of both MVFHR and Journey of Hope, as well as a speaker for Catholics Against Capital Punishment, the Catholic dioceses in Montana and other Christian groups. She is also involved in Montana's Abolition Coalition, and recently spoke to Montana's Senate Judiciary Committee in support of a bill to abolish the state's death penalty. Marietta continues to travel around the world with her Christian message of forgiveness.

I know when I share my experience it is a powerful story, and people are deeply moved. God redeems Susie's suffering and death by making it a gift of life for other people. This is not the script that I wanted for my life but it was written by the Holy Spirit and therefore it is giving life.

In the year following Susie's disappearance, I reached a point where I was ready to give up my belief in God because of the many mitigating circumstances of the night Susie was taken. How was the kidnapper successful in taking her away? Why did no one hear or notice him? And why would a loving God allow this? This churned over and over in my mind, and I began to doubt whether God existed. "Perhaps," I thought, "God is just a psychological crutch that some person dreamed up long ago to keep us all in line." I was at the end of my rope and ready to give up a belief in God. But the more my reasoning moved in that direction, the more my spirit was saying,

"Wait! I need the hope that God gives. God is the only One I can count on in this situation." I then had an image of being pushed to the edge of a precipice, looking down and seeing that it was bottomless, dark, and terrifying. Instinctively I knew that I had to make an act of faith in a God that I couldn't see, hear, feel, or understand. And I did. At that moment I had a powerful, mystical experience of being in the presence of God.

Without my faith, I would not have survived the agonizing months after Susie was abducted, or the trauma of learning about the depravity and torture she was subjected to. My faith gives me the consolation of knowing that whatever violence happened to Susie, it is not her reality now. Susie went on to a glorious place and celebrates life in the arms of God. This was confirmed for me a number of years ago when I was with my mother during the last week of her life. A couple of days before she died, she woke in the middle of the night and saw Susie dancing at the foot of her bed, waving and saying, "Pretty soon, Grandma, we will be together again." That is the image I hold of Susie.

***

"Without being forgiven, released from the consequences of what we have done, our capacity to act would . . . be confined to a single deed from which we could never recover," wrote Hannah Arendt in 1958. "We would remain the victims of its consequences forever, not unlike the sorcerer's apprentice, who lacked the magic formula to break the spell" (1998: 237). Joe Avila and Marietta Jaeger Lane have explored the painful truth of this wise dictum, trying to break the spell of their respective roles as offender and victim. Each of them have taken what happened seriously, as Tutu puts it, yet continually work on "drawing out the sting in the memory that threatens to poison our entire existence." This work has, as Hammarskjold knew, entailed sacrifice, but has also helped break the "chain of causality" in order to make genuine space for redemption.

5

WITNESSING IN WAR ZONES

Deconstructing Enmity

I tremble for our world. I do so not only from dire recall of the night-
mares wreaked in the wars of yesterday, but also from dreadful realization of today's possible nuclear destructiveness, and tomorrow's
even more damnable prospects. The past is prophetic in that it asserts
loudly that wars are poor chisels for carving out peaceful tomorrows.
One day we must come to see that peace is not merely a distant goal
that we seek, but a means by which we arrive at that goal.

—Dr. Martin Luther King, Jr.[1]

Armies expect casualties when they go to war. Those working for
peace in war zones have to expect the same.

—Christian Peacemaker Team member Tom Fox
to his children before his final trip to Iraq
(Brown, 2008: 205)

"Christ is our peace," wrote the author of the Epistle to the Ephesians,
"having broken down the dividing wall of enmity" (Eph 2:14,16).[2] The
New Testament sage understood that the consciousness of hostility
toward an "other" constitutes the most primal and deeply rooted charac-
teristic of the architecture of personal, communal, and national conflict.

---

1. From "The Casualties of the War in Vietnam," delivered February 25, 1967, at the
Nation Institute in Los Angeles (text at www.aavw.org/special_features/speeches_speech_
king02.html). This was the first time Dr. King had publicly articulated his opposition to the
war in Indochina, and it paved the way for his more famous "Beyond Vietnam" address less
than two months later (see volume I, chapter 2, n. 2).

2. See our examination of this key theological assertion in volume I, chapter 4.

And enmity is certainly a necessary condition for the waging of war. In his psychological analysis of our "love of hatred," Ofer Zur reminds us that "guns do not kill, heads do. Before we create the gun or the bomb, we have first to envision the destruction of the enemy in our minds" (1991: 345).

We have seen the politics of enmity dramatically played out in global terms since the events of September 11, 2001, both in the actions of terrorists and the war against terrorism. But "hate cannot drive out hate," warned Dr. King—"only love can." Myrna Bethke and James Loney, inspired by the legacy of King and the moral vision of the New Testament, represent a growing minority of North American Christians who are beginning to defect from the culture of enmity. Bethke and Loney were, in a sense, both victims of war, but also offenders, in the sense that they were citizens of countries involved in military invasions. Yet they transgressed the strictures of wartime's absolute demand for national loyalty by traveling to war zones to seek the human face of the "enemy." Their witness suggests how disciples might live into the conviction that Christ has dismantled the dividing wall of hostility.

5A. Myrna Bethke
of September Eleventh Families for Peaceful Tomorrows

Myrna Bethke, left, in Afghanistan, 2002.

Photo credit: United Methodist News Service.
Courtesy of Myrna Bethke, used with permission

Marietta Jaeger's journey began with an intensely personal violation followed by a deeply private struggle, which slowly led to public political witness (above, 4B). Myrna Bethke's story began with a spectacularly political crime, to which she offered a profoundly personal response. The abduction and torture of Marietta's daughter took place in secret. But the whole world witnessed the killing of more than three thousand people in the September 11, 2001, terrorist attacks on the World Trade Center towers and the Pentagon. One of those victims was Myrna's thirty-seven-year-old brother, Bill. While

9/11 was used as a call to global war by U.S. leaders, some family members of those killed in the attacks made poignant pleas that violence not be done in their loved ones' names, and instead turned their grief into actions for peace. Myrna was among them. We interviewed her on April 30, 2007.

Myrna is the oldest child of five siblings and grew up in the United Methodist Church.

> My mom led my Girls Scouts' troop and was always pushing boundaries, looking for different experiences and encouraging us to try new things. This early exposure gave me the foundation to experiment, take risks, and be inclusive.
>
> My call to ministry was slow and unfolding. In high school, I wondered about becoming a pastor, but to that point had never experienced a female minister. I didn't know it was possible until a woman was appointed to our local church while doing her field education work in seminary.
>
> Two experiences in seminary helped lay a foundation for me to respond to 9/11: studying the book of Job and issues of theodicy in the world; and doing my clinical pastoral education work in oncology in the early 1980s (when cancer was more of a death sentence than it is now). During this time, I wrestled deeply with these issues, asking: "Do we really believe that God is bigger than anything we can come up with?"

Ordained in 1982 as a United Methodist pastor, Myrna has served in a variety of churches in New Jersey, most recently as senior pastor at the United Methodist Church of Red Bank. Prior to 9/11 she had worked with various peace and justice organizations, and chaired the Urban Ministries Committee of her Conference; she was not, however, significantly involved in protesting the first Gulf War. Working through a significant professional conflict with a colleague showed her the importance of consensus and the meaning of figuring out a "win-win solution." Another influence was her appointment as pastor at Freehold United Methodist Church, which had just completed a conflict resolution process with the Alban Institute, a nonprofit organization that helps resource and guide congregations through conflict. "I was very fortunate to be working in a church that took conflict and healing very seriously, because soon after I came, 9/11 happened."

i. Facing the Rubble in New York

On Tuesday, September 11, 2001, two commercial airplanes were hijacked and flown into the World Trade Center in New York City;

soon after, both buildings collapsed. A third plane was crashed into the Pentagon in Washington, D.C., and a fourth went down in a field in Pennsylvania.[3]

> I watched in numbing horror the unfolding events of that day as plane after plane crashed, wondering where it would end. I did not know in the first few moments as I watched, just how personal this tragedy was to become. My family joined all of those you saw on the news . . . posting pictures of my brother on the streets of New York City, visiting the area hospitals . . . posting e-mail messages with his picture.
>
> It became clear after about a day of checking the e-mail messages that everyone was looking for employees of Cantor Fitzgerald and employees of Marsh & McLennan, where my brother worked. No one was hearing from those who worked on the ten floors occupied by these two companies in Tower One. We knew that if my brother had been in his office, he was in that area. It was on Thursday that we received confirmation that my youngest brother, Bill, was on the ninety-fifth floor of the first tower hit—in the direct path of Flight 11. The only "official" confirmation of his death to this day is his silence (Potorti, 2003: 130).

Though Bill's remains have still not been found, a computer card swipe confirmed he was in his office at the time of the attack.

Freehold United Methodist Church is about forty miles outside of New York City. Some members worked in lower Manhattan, and everyone in the congregation knew someone who had been personally affected by the attacks. The church immediately opened its doors for all who wanted to come and pray, and during the days following 9/11 Myrna continued to perform her pastoral duties while learning her brother's fate.

> I did not feel that my response had to be compartmentalized. Dealing with the loss of my brother personally did not keep me from responding to my professional work. I knew I could work on the loss of my brother at the same time that we, as the church, were working corporately on the larger tragedy—because isn't that who we are as the church? We are supposed to know what to do in these situations so that we can respond in a matter fitting to who we are as God's people, and not just give a knee-jerk reaction.

---

3. The literature on the attacks is voluminous, as are conspiracy and counter-conspiracy theories concerning the real causes, culprits, and consequences. We recommend Chomsky (2001); Hersh (2004); and Griffin (2006).

It felt like we, as the church, knew what to do. We gathered for worship on that Tuesday evening; it was the place and time for raw emotions, grief, and rage. We read Psalm 137 in its entirety, including the last verse about dashing our enemies' babies' heads against the rocks. We read this as lifting up our rage to God and shaking our fists—not as a call to action. We needed a place and a biblical context for grieving and raging. The next night, we came together again and spoke of healing and shared communion.

A number of congregants lost cousins, or more distant relatives, but I was most directly affected. I wonder how my personal response shaped the reaction of others in the congregation. The congregants were very supportive of the pathways laid out in terms of our worship and my own response. I never heard any vindictiveness or questions of, "Don't you want to get the people who did this?"

Myrna presided over the memorial service for her brother and three other employees from his company. But she also longed for a service led by someone else that would aid her personal healing.

Bill and I did not get to see each other often because of the distance between where we lived, yet we had common interests and enjoyed having fun together. He died just a few weeks shy of his thirty-eighth birthday. We had two services for Bill. I led the memorial for his division of the Marsh & McLennan firm, which previously was located in Princeton and had been transferred to the World Trade Towers just four months before 9/11. I was not involved in leading the other memorial service, and was hoping it would be a time for me to process some of my loss. But it did not meet my needs.

Later, I figured out what I missed most during the funeral for my brother—hearing his name hooked to our liturgy. So I worked it out with a friend to do that for me. My friend and I went to the beach in Sandy Hook, which has a view of the New York skyline and he read the words for me and named my brother Bill in our liturgy. Now, twice a year I go back to the beach in Sandy Hook and put flowers in the ocean. I have learned that even when things do not go the way they are supposed to, I am responsible to figure out what I need for my own healing.

President George W. Bush, a Methodist layman, modeled the classic response of retribution: personalizing the evil of 9/11 in Osama bin Laden and launching massive retaliatory strikes against Afghanistan simply because bin Laden was reputed to be hiding there. In contrast, Methodist pastor Bethke modeled a creative and restorative response.

> Once the immediate needs of 9/11 were taken care of, I found myself longing to make a response that would work towards redemption and restoration. I was fairly certain, at that point, that we were going to bomb Afghanistan and was asking myself, "What can I personally do to stop this?"
>
> On October 7th, the bombing of Afghanistan began. It was my brother Bill's birthday, and that year it also happened to be Worldwide Communion Sunday. I came home from church to the news that we were dropping bombs. I felt so sad, and as a 9/11 family member, felt personal responsibility for the attack on Afghanistan. I was overwhelmed and wondered if there were other 9/11 family members who felt as I did.

There were. David Potorti explains:

> Because the killing was being undertaken in the names of their loved ones and their families, they felt something else: ownership. This war would be their war, fought in their names. This gave them the will to speak out. And it was by speaking out that they became known to their communities—and to each other. If September 11 united them in loss, it was the bombing of Afghanistan that united them in their desire to attain justice without killing more innocent people. (Potorti, 2003: 21)

On Valentine's Day 2002, September Eleventh Families for Peaceful Tomorrows was founded, inspired by the dictum of Dr. King.

Their mission statement reads, "Peaceful Tomorrows is an organization founded by family members of those killed on September 11th who have united to turn our grief into actions for peace. By developing and advocating nonviolent options and actions in the pursuit of justice, we hope to break the cycles of violence engendered by war and terrorism. Acknowledging our common experience with all people affected by violence throughout the world, we work to create a safer and more peaceful world for everyone" (www.peacefultomorrows.org).

Peaceful Tomorrows represents more than a hundred family members of September 11 victims, and gave Myrna an avenue to take personal responsibility for the war.

> As family members of those killed on 9/11, we have moral authority because no one can say to us, "You don't know how it is." This has

given us a sense of responsibility to speak out. Because of our experience, people listen more carefully to what we say. Even if they do not always agree with me, I consider it a compliment when someone says, "You have given me something to think about."

ii. Facing the Rubble in Afghanistan

In spring 2002, Myrna was invited to go on an interfaith clergy delegation to Afghanistan as a representative of Peaceful Tomorrows, organized by Global Exchange.[4] She was interested in going, but felt the choice was not hers alone.

> I also felt it was my parents' decision. And I would have completely understood if they responded, "Are you kidding me? We cannot deal with the possibility of such a trip after losing Billy." But when I told my father about the invitation to go to Afghanistan, his response was, "What help do you need from us to get there?" I was very grateful and surprised at my father's generosity and support after just having lost his youngest son. Freehold Congregation was also very supportive and raised the entire amount needed for me to go to Afghanistan.

The interfaith delegation focused on ways to support projects in Afghanistan that were rebuilding schools, clinics, and mosques destroyed by U.S. bombing.

> One of the most powerful experiences in Afghanistan was spending time with a beautiful little girl named Amina. We spent the day together playing and drawing pictures. Then in the evening, I learned her story. One morning, Amina had gotten up to make tea for her family. She was in the back of the house getting water when a bomb hit the front half of the house. Amina lost her entire family in that instant; she was the only survivor. When she spoke to our group she stood and listed the names of all of her family members who had been killed. I found myself thinking, "No eight-year-old child should have to do this!"
>
> As I was listening to Amina, a memory came flooding back. Two weeks after 9/11, I was talking with my father on the phone when we

---

4. Members of Peaceful Tomorrows have also traveled to Iraq, Japan, Korea, India, Turkey, Italy, and Britain.

were interrupted. "The state police just arrived," he said, "and they want me to give a DNA sample." I felt so horrible that my father had to do this in order to identify his son. In Afghanistan, these two events powerfully came together. It became clear to me that we are all called to build a world in which parents and children do not have to name their dead in this way.

Myrna also recognizes the power of evil in the world, and touched that briefly during her time in Afghanistan.

Our group had been wandering as tourists one day, and we went to one of the royal palaces in the outskirts of Kabul. It was in ruins because it had been shelled so many times. We went in and unexpectedly came upon a room that was freshly painted and cleaned. There was no dust or sign of ruin. Suddenly we were surrounded by soldiers; it was frightening and we wondered how it happened so quickly. Our translator said, "We are okay, but it is time to go." The soldiers were leering and laughing at us, saying, "This is where bin Laden comes when he makes plans."

I also sensed the power of evil when we were allowed to walk in the stadium in downtown Kabul where the Taliban has executed people; the victims' blood is still crying out. I speak of these two incidents because we cannot underestimate that there truly are people working for the power of evil in our world. In our work for peace, we are not always going to succeed, but the question that keeps me going is: "What defines me—the action of terrorists or the love of God?"

What was cemented for me through 9/11 and my trip to Afghanistan is my belief that God is with us. The Word has become flesh and dwells among us. That is the foundation from which we live, and we are called to follow the example of Christ. Paul asks, "If God is for us, who can be against us?" (Rom 8:31) Even when the worst happens, God is still bigger.

Myrna continues to work on the difficult practices of forgiveness, healing, and reconciliation, striving to be a realistic peacemaker in a world corrupted by abuse of power and violence.

I strive to be up front with conflict resolution, but after 9/11 people listen differently to me. My churches develop behavior covenants outlining how we will behave with each other in our meetings. I believe that our behavior in a church meeting is just as important as our behavior on the world stage. If we behave nonviolently there, I believe it shapes the world a little.

I separate forgiveness from reconciliation. Forgiveness is something I can personally do in order to be free from the hurtful act that was perpetrated. Lament is central because when we are hurt and violated, we need a place and a space for grieving and rage. Only after that can we move towards healing and forgiveness, which for me are intertwined. The act of forgiving is a release, which can happen for me as an individual and does not require a response from the other. Reconciliation, however, is a whole different matter.

I am not sure how I would respond if the people responsible for 9/11 were willing to talk. When I am in situations like this, my first response is to figure out how we can move forward, asking, "What is plan B?" But plan B is too simple; in the case of 9/11 we may need to ask, "What is plan Q? And how are we going to work together and live together on the same planet?"

Peaceful Tomorrows has subsequently been nominated for the Nobel Peace Prize. On the fifth anniversary of 9/11, the group organized the first international gathering of families affected by terrorism and war. It brought together more than thirty individuals from war zones around the world who are devoted to cooperation, healing, and reconciliation. The conference established an international network of women and men who have been personally affected by violence, yet who have rejected the idea of retaliating with further violence.

After Myrna returned from Afghanistan she was invited to speak at the Shiite mosque in her community of Freehold.

I am very grateful for my ongoing relationship with people at this mosque! Our relationship is one of the blessings that came out of the tragedy. Before 9/11, Freehold had an active Jewish/Christian clergy association. A month after 9/11, Islamic clergy joined us, and have become an integral part of the Freehold Clergy Association.

Myrna continues a strong relationship with the mosque, regularly taking her confirmation classes from Red Bank for a Ramadan dinner. This is one of the concrete ways that Myrna now practices peacemaking: by expanding the table and bringing together her parishioners with her Shiite friends.

The Shias have a long history of lament tradition, and I have also done some work on the lament tradition in Christianity and Judaism. After I spoke at our local mosque, a woman came to me crying, saying, "We thought only the poetry of Arabic could express our lament. Today you taught us that you could lament in English as well."

5B. James Loney of Christian Peacemaker Teams

James Loney, at a public vigil for security detainees, Tahrir Square, Baghdad, February 2004.

Photo credit: Christian Peacemaker Teams, used with permission

On November 26, 2005, four members of Christian Peacemaker Teams stepped out of Baghdad's Umm al-Qura mosque into the bright sunshine. It was the last sunlight they would see in four months. Moments later their vehicle was hijacked while guns were held to their heads. The captors later identified themselves as the Swords of Righteousness Brigade. Through videos and statements sent to an Arabic-language television network, the captors threatened to kill the four men unless all security detainees were released. The four kidnapped men were Canadians James Loney and Harmeet Singh Sooden; American Tom Fox; and British citizen Norman Kember.

Christian Peacemaker Teams (CPT) was founded in 1988 by Mennonite and Brethren activists to deepen and intensify Christian nonviolent resistance to war and injustice. Today, with broad ecumenical support, Christian Peacemaker Teams are deployed in crisis situations around the world, ready to risk injury and death by intervening in violent situations with the power of nonviolence.[5]

In October 2002, CPT began a long-term presence in Iraq, anticipating that the United States would invade the country in response to 9/11.

---

5. See www.cpt.org. A detailed account of the hostage episode related here is found in Brown (2008).

Members stood with Iraqi civilians as the bombing began in March 2003. The primary focus of CPT following the invasion was to document and focus attention on the abuse of security detainees and the denial of their basic legal and human rights by the United States. In Iraq, CPT members are the only unarmed international workers left outside of the heavily fortified U.S. security zone near Baghdad.

i. A Helplessness That Leads to God

There was an unprecedented international outcry after the abduction of the four CPT workers, including public appeals from significant Muslim leaders for their release. But on March 9, 2006, after three and a half months in captivity, Tom Fox's body was found on the streets of Baghdad. He had been shot in the head and chest. Two weeks later, after 118 days of captivity, James, Harmeet, and Norman were released by British forces without violence, their captors having fled.

James and his life-partner, Dan Hunt, are part of the Catholic Worker Community in Toronto (see chapter 4, n. 8). Their committed relationship goes back to the 1990s, before James's involvement with CPT. James first went on a CPT delegation to Iraq in 2003 before the war began. A year later, he traveled back to Iraq for ten weeks. In November 2005, James went to Iraq on a short-term delegation, expecting to be there for just ten days. For James's safety while in captivity, his relationship with Dan was hidden from the public—an excruciating experience of invisibility for Dan as he waited for news of his beloved. We interviewed James in Toronto on May 30, 2006, nine weeks after he was released from his four-month captivity.

> We were handcuffed and chained for twenty-three hours a day. The guards brought us food three times a day, and would usually come when we needed to use the bathroom. Other than that, they would only check on us occasionally, so there were long hours when we were on our own. The guns, the vicious dog barking in the next room, the stifled screams of another captive, these were moments of terror. The times I had the greatest fear were when I prayed the most. But I was not afraid all of the time. We settled in to a kind of ordinary time, as absurd as that sounds, and it became much more an act of will for me to pray in an intentional way.
>
> Being kidnapped seemed a very remote possibility, but once we were in captivity, the possibility of being released seemed even more remote. The more difficult struggle was not that something would happen to me or us, but whether I should do something to take control of the situation. Should I try to escape and risk everything? Just

before we were kidnapped, I read a book called "Bitter Embrace," which is about the colonization of a Cree Community in Saskatchewan. It is a story of terrible suffering. One of the events I remember most vividly is about a Cree man who was a recent convert to Christianity. He and his seven-year-old son were going to visit relatives across the river and got in a motor boat just above rapids. The man pulled on the motor but it would not start. The current was pulling them towards the rapids. The man started praying to God, reciting Psalms of deliverance, but they were pulled into the rapids and died. There were oars in the boat . . . but the man didn't use them. During our four months in captivity, there were moments, what seemed like opportunities for escape, and I would question, "Is this the time, is the oar in the boat right now, should I be acting?" Those were very painful struggles, and much more agonizing than fear. I suppose it is this kind of helplessness that leads us to God in the end.

Captivity is an experience of all kinds of deprivation. For us, this included the written word. We did not have song books, prayer books, or a Bible. All we had was what we could remember. At Tom's initiative, we had daily Bible studies. Each day one of us would pick a Bible passage from memory and recite it as best we could. Tom then posed four questions that he had used with young people: What is the meaning of this passage? How does it fit with my experience? What is confusing or troubling about this passage? And how might it change my life?

We were very diverse in our theological backgrounds. Tom was a Quaker; Norman, a Baptist; Harmeet was raised culturally as a Sikh and went to Christian boarding school in England; and I am a Catholic. We had very different points of view and vigorous discussion. We closed our Bible study with a time of worship and prayer in which each of us spoke about how we were feeling. These ways of being church together helped us shift the mental tables somewhat. The act of praying together for our captors (Tom called it "holding them in the Light") helped us to have a lifeline to their dignity as human beings. Recognizing their dignity protected us in two ways. It helped the captors see our humanity, which was in our interest because it is harder to kill someone who is a person to you. And it protected us from either accepting the role of powerless victim or being corrupted by rage. But we never prayed in our captor's presence, mostly because we did not want to be perceived as trying to evangelize.

The leader of their group, who we called Medicine Man because he brought Norman's blood pressure pills, spoke broken English. The other captors spoke even less English, and we did not speak any Arabic, so we had very limited communication together. I do not think they knew of CPT, and my sense is that they abducted us because we were Westerners from whom they might make money to fund their insurgency. We established early on that we were "Esau Salaam" (peace Christians) who did not believe in using guns, and who were in their country to help the Iraqi people. All of our captors seemed to respect this except for one, and aside from one incident there was never any hatred directed toward us because we were Christians. One of our captors gave us an hour-long lecture on why we should convert to Islam. At least four of our captors were religiously motivated and had a profound sense of religious identity. They prayed five times a day as their religion requires and were deeply rooted in an Islamic way of understanding the world and their actions. They believed that by protecting their country from an invader, they were being faithful to what the Qur'an mandates. In a proscribed sort of way, we got to know three guards intimately. We had an intuitive sense of what motivated them and what their character was like. It is clear to me that they had a rationale for what they were doing, but they did not enjoy guarding us. Near the end of our time in captivity, the guards would point to our handcuffs and say, "we are handcuffed too." We often asked them when we would be released. They would answer, "We don't know. When you are free, we will be free too." To me this summed up the paradox of the whole situation.

I believe the guards were as bored as we were. But they asked me, "If the U.S. invaded Canada, wouldn't you fight back with guns?" I answered, "No, because I don't believe in guns. I would resist, but not that way," to which one of them scoffed. But what is the difference between their rationale and that of the American or British soldier? They are all working from the same narrative that justifies what they are doing. People rarely take up guns because they are "bad"; they always have a rationale.

Except for their second week in captivity, when Norman and Tom were separated from Harmeet and James, the four were always held in the same room. Tom was taken from them on February 12, and the captors told them that he had been released. The three remaining captives tried to remain hopeful, but gradually came to assume the worst. Early in the morning of March 23, 2006, James heard a door slam.

This was unusual because the captors were never up before 10 o'clock. Then fifteen minutes later, we heard the sound of a tank, boots running, voices in English shouting, "Open the door." We knew we were safe when we heard the soldiers coming up the stairs. We learned later that the guards had fled from the house. The British soldiers cut the chains around our hands and feet. We gathered our things and were escorted outside. In the space of about fifty feet between the door of the house and the tank, I saw a palm tree and brilliant blue sky for the first time in 118 days. We were escorted through a gauntlet of soldiers to the tank.

I saw Medicine Man blindfolded, facing a wall wearing a white gown—probably what he'd slept in that night. I didn't recognize him at first because he looked so different. When we were in captivity he was always in charge, wearing a business suit and well-shaven, with his cell phone and gun tucked into his waistband. He called the shots. Now his face had fallen. He was bewildered and powerless with armed soldiers surrounding him. I stopped for a moment and, not knowing what to say, I put my hand on his shoulder. He jumped, and I felt bad because I startled him. I wanted to say his name but I didn't even know what it was; I wish now that I had thought to say my name so that he would have known who it was that touched him. I said a short prayer for him and then a soldier brought me to the tank.

My understanding is that Medicine Man was captured and told U.S. intelligence where we were being held. I also surmise that he called our guards and told them they should get out of there. Allowing the guards to escape was a calculated risk on the part of the military authorities because the guards could have killed us first. I am grateful they were given the opportunity to leave, however, because I think they would have fought if they had not been given the option to slip out.

Shortly after their rescue, James, Harmeet, and Norman were allowed to return to their respective homes. They were very grateful to be released from captivity and reunited with their families and friends. Their joy was severely sobered, however, by their grief over the loss of Tom, and for his family and community. The three surviving captives were heavily, and falsely, criticized by North American conservative churches and media for not expressing public gratitude to Coalition troops for rescuing them.

Obviously, given the fact that we were in Iraq to challenge the war, it is a paradox that we were rescued by soldiers. And since CPT's work has been protesting and exposing the house raids and the illegal holding and treatment of detainees, it is a paradox that it was a detainee that gave the information that got us out of captivity. These are some of the contradictions we face trying to be peacemakers in a war zone where nothing is clear.

Our hope, and CPT's hope, was always that the men who kidnapped us would have a change of heart and let us go. That never happened. And that is good in a way, to have that paradox, because we might be tempted into an easy, self-righteous position that nonviolence always "works." It doesn't always work. But it made me very sad to see these battle-hardened Special Forces guys, each laden with heavy gear, each risking their lives to serve their country in the best way that they can. I probably wouldn't be sitting here today talking with you if it wasn't for them. So I was incredibly grateful and deeply sad at the same time. Some men with guns came and took us. And then some bigger guys with bigger guns came and took them. We are free, but the gun is still in control. And everybody who's holding a gun thinks they are the good guy doing the right thing.

ii. Getting in the Way of War

James was an activist for many years before his involvement with CPT. His commitment to nonviolence flowed out of his work with the Catholic Worker, a Christian anarchist and pacifist movement founded by Dorothy Day and Peter Maurin in the 1930s in New York City. There are Catholic Worker communities around the world providing meals, clothing, medical aid, and housing for homeless people, while also challenging poverty and injustice. The Catholic Worker rejects all forms of violence, and sees war-making both as theft of resources from the poor and contrary to Jesus' teachings about love of enemy.

James, Dan, and a third gay man, William Payne, started the Toronto Catholic Worker in 1990. While living in community with people who were homeless, James witnessed the consequences of poverty and felt challenged to look more deeply at the structures of inequity. This encouraged him to move deeper into activism and advocacy.

When I learned about CPT, I saw it as a very important experiment in nonviolence. At the Mennonite World Conference in 1984, Ron Sider called on people to take the same risks in peacemaking that soldiers take in war. CPT grew out of that challenge, exploring ways of living out the Christian mandate of nonviolence by moving beyond just saying no to war. For me it was the next logical step to take part in this experiment.

James took the CPT training in 2000 and became a reservist, a three-year commitment to participate in one of the CPT projects for at least two weeks each year. In August 2005, James became the program co-coordinator for CPT Canada.

The CPT motto amends a discipleship motif by inviting Christians not only to follow Jesus "on the way," but to "get *in* the way" of violence. CPT teams work with communities that are affected by lethal violence. What they do varies from conflict to conflict. CPT's general aim is to complement and amplify the voices of their grassroots partners through public witness, physical accompaniment, nonviolent direct action, documenting human rights abuses, community organizing, and building international networks of solidarity. CPT will only go to places where they have been invited and where the U.S. or Canadian governments have a role in the violence.

We are prepared to intervene in a potentially violent scenario, such as at a blockade or checkpoint. When soldiers and civilians are together, and the civilians are at some risk, we interpose our bodies to try to diffuse and de-escalate the situation. Most of our work, however, consists of networking, meeting with people, planning, and building relationships with local activists. A large part of CPT training is accompaniment work, where we learn how to use our physical presence as a third party in strategic ways to help protect those who are at risk for their human rights and peace work. We also focus on human rights documentation and how to plan and organize nonviolent direct actions. So before we were kidnapped we had begun to document the torture of Iraqi citizens by their own government.

When CPT is invited into an area of violence, our first task is to analyze the situation by researching the roots of the conflict and the structures that have created and are maintaining it. We also determine how power is distributed and how it is being exercised. We believe that you cannot be neutral in a situation of injustice. We work in partnership with those affected by lethal violence to try to correct the imbalance of power by exercising the power of nonviolence. We support the building of "people power" on the ground, and solidarity in the local and international community. Our work is thus both violence reduction and power building.

CPT has deployed teams in more than two dozen different locations around the world over the last twenty years, each context and conflict with distinct complexities.[6] In war zones, both victimized communities and

---

6. For a history and accounts of CPT work over this period, see Kern (2008); Brown (2005).

the nongovernmental organizations (NGOs) working on their behalf rely heavily on the work of CPT.

> In Colombia or Palestine, our international passports offer some protection for citizens, but in Iraq our presence as internationals does not afford any safety. In fact, the Iraqis who work with us are at risk. It is a very delicate stance to figure out if our presence is more helpful than it is harmful.
>
> The power map in Iraq has become more complex since the American and British occupation. Now Iraq has many powerful entities battling for control: a fledgling government of its own, with Iranian and American influence; different kinds of insurgency groups; a Kurdish semirepublic in the north; and Shia and Sunni constituencies and conflicts. The local security force is the Iraqi police, and the Ministry of the Interior has eleven different security forces, all with their own prisons. It is a difficult terrain of violence and counterviolence.
>
> We do not come to the conflict zone with solutions—this is one of CPT's unwavering commitments. We also do not provide nonviolent direct action training for local folks unless they request it. We come to support the work that is already being done by local people. Typically situations in which we intervene are so volatile that mediation isn't an option, and civil society groups are in danger. Our hope is to provide space and safety for grassroots groups to have dialogue and to put nonviolent alternatives in place.

In all practices of peacemaking, activists are questioned as to whether their work is effective. Loved ones raise real concerns about personal risk and sacrifice. The church, courts, and media often ridicule peacemakers for their "radical" positions and actions of nonviolence. Yet rarely does the majority of the church question the effectiveness of war-making.

> CPT can sometimes be dramatically effective, especially in a micro context. In Colombia, for example, there was a mining labor organizer who was arrested. This happens a lot, where organizers are harassed and silenced with false, trumped-up charges, and they sit in jail for a long time. In this case, this organizer had been working with CPT, and CPT was able to call upon an international network it had built up to respond to these kinds of situations. When the Colombian authorities began to receive inquiries from around the world, they released him and dropped the charges. In Ontario, we accompanied a blockade that the Anishinaabe community of Grassy Narrows put

up in order to protect their land from being clear-cut. They ran the blockade, they stood in front of the trucks—we just stood by with our cameras and notebooks and brought a lot of outside attention to what was happening there. There was never any violence, not from the police or from the loggers. The Grassy blockaders attribute that to our presence. Another classic incident happened about five years ago in Hebron. A group of Palestinians organized a disciplined nonviolent protest against a curfew. They wanted to do their Friday prayers at the checkpoint. They came down the hill towards the boundary between the Israeli-controlled and Palestinian-controlled parts of Hebron. Israeli soldiers had assumed firing positions behind giant cement blocks, their guns were cocked and ready to fire. Sara Reschly and other CPT members were in front of the nonviolent protestors. Sara stood right in front of an Israeli soldier with her arms outstretched, blocking him firing at the protestors. The media was there, a picture was taken that went all around the world. The soldiers—just boys, really—did not fire. They calmed down and the tension de-escalated, and the Palestinians were able to pray at the checkpoint. This happens rarely and a lot of work goes into such moments, but it is a model of what we hope can happen.

The question of effectiveness is something that my father and I talk about. Before I went to Iraq in November, he told me, "Why are you going? You are not going to accomplish anything. Those people have been fighting for centuries and they will fight for centuries more. What can you do?" But in Amman, Jordan, when we met with the Red Cross and the UN Human Rights office, I was pleasantly surprised by how much they value CPT's work. These two organizations cannot be in Iraq because they have assessed it is too dangerous. They are trying to do their humanitarian work from remote control in Amman. CPT is one of very few NGOs, if not the only one, that is still working in Iraq. The Red Cross and the UN Human Rights office told us they read our reports religiously, and value our perspective.

We are prepared and able to take risks that the UN or Red Cross can't. Before the kidnapping, we traveled around freely in Iraq and went to places they could not dream of going. Is our work in Iraq effective? I suppose, at the least, it is a contribution. I wouldn't make any claims beyond that.

CPT, through their accompaniment, documentation, and human rights work began hearing stories of the abuse of Iraqi detainees. CPT helped to break the story of the abuse and torture of prisoners held in the Abu

Ghraib prison. Graphic pictures showing U.S. military police personnel in the act of abusing prisoners came to public attention on April 28, 2004.

> Information about Abu Ghraib was leaking out through a number of channels, soldiers were circulating pictures, and it was just a matter of time before the truth came out. I was there a few weeks before the story broke, and was hearing rumors of sexual torture. It was difficult to confirm these stories, and we wondered if they were "urban myths." But we continued investigating and reporting on the condition of detainees. When a front page story in the New York Times told the truth about Abu Ghraib, it was a lesson for me: if we chip away at issues consistently, we will eventually expose the truth.
>
> The purpose of CPT is to work in disciplined ways to perfect peacemaking, in the same manner that armies work in disciplined ways to perfect war-making. We need constantly to be learning and becoming more effective. We do not have the luxury of being ineffective, because lives are at stake. This is a spiritual struggle. I've occasionally heard CPTers say it is more important to be faithful than successful. I think it's easy to say this when your situation is comfortable and you have all the necessities of life. But when your children are dying from poverty or oppression and when violence is raging around you, there is an incredible urgency to be effective.

The people involved in the dangerous and taxing peace work of CPT draw deeply on a spiritual well, searching for guidance, courage, forgiveness, and reconciliation.

> It is hard for me to imagine doing this work without faith. On a personal level, faith offers me a system of meaning and enables me to take risks. It also securely lodges me in a much larger community. This kind of resistance work has been going on from the time of Abraham and Sarah. It is this community of saints that gives me strength.
>
> It is not simply my personal belief in Jesus that will save me. Faith is also the shared experience of the church, the people of God together. Faith gives us a place to meet and a tradition which provides songs to sing and stories to tell. We share a vision that is bigger than any individual. Together we have the resources of prayer and the Holy Spirit, to carry us while reminding us that our peacemaking work is not about individual success or ego. Faith is about God's call and being servants of the Gospel. It is an incredible richness that I cherish.

While in captivity, forgiveness was something we talked about at different times, but curiously it seemed like a remote, abstract discussion. We spoke of forgiveness in general but not about the circumstance we were in, perhaps because our situation was so sensitive. During this time, I wrestled with the meaning of forgiveness and reconciliation, and came to understand that they are different things. Forgiveness is a movement in the person who has been offended or hurt. Repentance or contrition is a movement in the person who has offended. The meeting of these two is when reconciliation can happen. For the victim, forgiveness is a necessary doorway to the possibility of reconciliation. Whether or not reconciliation occurs, however, forgiveness can liberate the victim from what was imposed on them. In that sense, it is a movement of healing within the victim that can ultimately lead to healing in the offender.

We don't know who killed Tom. I only know the faces but not names of the people who abducted us and of the men who held us. I assume it is the same group—those that kidnapped us and those that killed Tom—although it certainly couldn't have been the guards who were on duty the night Tom was killed. When I think of Tom's family, his Friends Meeting, and how profoundly he was loved, it becomes an audacious thing to say, "I forgive you." Forgiveness is a continual act of faith that requires placing oneself in the hands of God. In a way, forgiveness was integral to the whole process, something I had to do every day in order to see the humanity of the captors. But to actually say the words, "I forgive you," while sitting face-to-face with our captors? I don't know. It would be easier for me to imagine doing that if I could see the suffering and humanity in them. If the words come they will come from God as a gift. God provides grace in God's time; all I can do is be open to it.

I would very much like to meet and talk with Medicine Man. I would like to understand his life, why he kidnapped us and the details surrounding our captivity and release. Apparently he is in custody with the American army and at some point he will be turned over to the Iraqi authorities. Of course, a meeting with Medicine Man seems unlikely. These things are in God's hands.

On December 10, 2006, James, Harmeet, and Norman held a press conference in London where they released the following statement of forgiveness:

We three, members of a Christian Peacemaker Teams (CPT) delegation to Iraq, were kidnapped on November 26, 2005, and held for 118 days before being freed by British and American forces on March 23, 2006. Our friend and colleague, Tom Fox, an American citizen and full-time member of the CPT team working in Baghdad at the time, was kidnapped with us and murdered on March 9, 2006. We are immensely sad that he is not sitting with us here today.

On behalf of our families and CPT, we thank you for attending this press conference today. It was on this day a year ago that our captors threatened to execute us unless their demands were met. This ultimatum, unknown to us at the time, was a source of extreme distress for our families, friends, and colleagues.

The deadline was extended by two days to December 10, which is International Human Rights Day. On this day, people all over the world will commemorate the adoption of the Universal Declaration of Human Rights by the UN General Assembly in 1948 by speaking out for all those whose human dignity is being violated by torture, arbitrary imprisonment, poverty, racism, oppression, or war.

We understand a number of men alleged to be our captors have been apprehended, charged with kidnapping, and are facing trial in the Central Criminal Court of Iraq. We have been asked by the police in our respective countries to testify in the trial. After much reflection upon our traditions, both Sikh and Christian, we are issuing this statement today.

We unconditionally forgive our captors for abducting and holding us. We have no desire to punish them. Punishment can never restore what was taken from us. What our captors did was wrong. They caused us, our families, and our friends great suffering. Yet we bear no malice towards them and have no wish for retribution. Should those who have been charged with holding us hostage be brought to trial and convicted, we ask that they be granted all possible leniency. We categorically lay aside any rights we may have over them.

In our view, the catastrophic levels of violence and the lack of effective protection of human rights in Iraq is inextricably linked to the U.S.-led invasion and occupation. As for many others, the actions of our kidnappers were part of a cycle of violence they themselves experienced. While this is no way justifies what the men charged with our kidnapping are alleged to have done, we feel this must be considered in any potential judgment.

Forgiveness is an essential part of Sikh, Christian, and Muslim teaching. Guru Nanak Dev Ji, the first of the Sikh Gurus said, "'For-giveness' is my mother . . ." and, "Where there is forgiveness, there is God." Jesus said, "For if you forgive those who sin against you, your heavenly Father will also forgive you." And of Prophet Mohammed

(Peace Be Upon Him) it is told that once, while preaching in the city of Ta'if, he was abused, stoned, and driven out of the city. An angel appeared to him and offered to crush the city between the two surrounding mountains if he ordered him to do so, whereupon the prophet (or Mohammed PBUH) said, "No. Maybe from them or their offspring will come good deeds."

Through the power of forgiveness, it is our hope that good deeds will come from the lives of our captors, and that we will all learn to reject the use of violence. We believe those who use violence against others are themselves harmed by the use of violence.

Kidnapping is a capital offence in Iraq and we understand that some of our captors could be sentenced to death. The death penalty is an irrevocable judgment. It erases all possibility that those who have harmed others, even seriously, can yet turn to good. We categorically oppose the death penalty.

By this commitment to forgiveness, we hope to plant a seed that one day will bear the fruits of healing and reconciliation for us, our captors, the peoples of Canada, New Zealand, the United Kingdom, the United States, and most of all, Iraq. We look forward to the day when the Universal Declaration of Human Rights is respected by all the world's people.[7]

**

The events of 9/11 and the war on terrorism that has ensued remind us of the burden of history: retribution cannot heal the wounds of violence, but only sows the seeds for further conflict. Myrna Bethke and James Loney, however, embraced Longfellow's famous invitation to "read the secret history of our enemies," and found there "sorrows and suffering enough to disarm all hostility." Their witness is another demonstration of the moral authority of the victim to redraw the map of possibility and of how regular citizens can break the cycle of violence engendered by war and terrorism.

---

7. Brown, 2008: 221ff. In March 2007, with participation from the FBI, the U.S. military, Scotland Yard, the Royal Canadian Mounted Police, and the New Zealand Police, the three CPT members held a video conference that was broadcast across sixteen time zones and five countries (New Zealand, the United States, Britain, Iraq, and Canada). At that time, they were informed that an undisclosed number of their captors were in U.S. custody and awaiting trial in the Central Criminal Court of Iraq for kidnapping. They have had no information since.

6

SOPHIA'S CHOICE

Women Facing the Beast

Christian hope begins where every other hope stands frozen stiff
before the face of the Unspeakable.
—Thomas Merton (1966: 5)

Through violence you may murder a murderer but you can't murder
murder. Through violence you may murder a liar but you can't establish truth. Through violence you may murder a hater, but you can't
murder hate. Darkness cannot put out darkness. Only light can do
that. . . .
—Martin Luther King, Jr. (Washington, 1986: 250)

In the prolegomenon to his peacemaking manifesto, the author of Ephesians declares: "With all wisdom (Gk. *sophia*) and insight God has made
known to us the mystery of the Divine will" (Eph 1:8).[1] He then prays
that God might grant the reader "a spirit of wisdom (Gk. *sophia*) and of
revelation" to understand and embrace the abolition of enmity embodied
in Christ (1:17). And it is "through the church that the diverse wisdom
(Gk. *sophia*) of God might now be made known to the Principalities and
Powers in the highest places" (Eph 3:10). This vision of evangelism as
militant engagement with the domination system—which often calls us
to "noncooperate with and expose the works of darkness" (Eph 5:11)—has
often been lost on a timid church. It is, however, understood well by the
women profiled in this chapter.

Three times Ephesians stresses the intimate relationship between the

---

1. Paul articulates a similar notion of God's wisdom (Gk. *sophia*) and "mystery" in 1 Cor
2:7. See our discussion of Ephesians in volume I, chapter 4.

"mysterious" vocation of peacemaking and the spirit of *sophia*. The image of divine Sophia as a woman is beloved in the Eastern Orthodox Church and is celebrated in the meditations of the great medieval Catholic mystic Hildegard of Bingen (see, e.g., Flanagan, 1998). In the last two decades, this tradition, marginalized in the Western church, has been recovered by Christian feminists.[2]

Its roots go all the way back to the Hebrew Bible, where the Hebrew word *chokhmah* (like the Greek *sophia*) is feminine. The most famous articulation is Proverbs 8-9, which portrays Wisdom as a female prophet trying to get the attention of the people of her village. Sophia urgently "takes her stand, crying out—on the heights, beside the way, at the crossroads, in front of the gates, at the entrance of the portals" (Prov 8:2). A woman would not typically have been seen in such prominent public places in the patriarchal culture of antiquity, where they were largely sequestered at home. But Lady Wisdom's message of justice (8:15f.) breaks gender taboos in its insistence. The writer offers a cosmic rationale: Sophia's truth not only preexists Creation (8:22-29), but indeed cocreated the world with God (8:30f.). In Proverbs 9, Sophia sets a table for a feast to which even the "simplest" are invited (9:1-5). Both images are profoundly maternal: the wise old crone demanding a hearing and the householder offering warm, nurturing hospitality.

"Wisdom is known by her children," said Jesus (Matt 11:19), invoking this very tradition.[3] Indeed, women have long held up the world by making peace in the home and the neighborhood, and by fiercely protecting their children at any cost. In many indigenous cultures women played special roles as peacemakers, intervening in conflicts and often declaring truces in war.[4] In U.S. history alone the cloud of witnesses is vast:

---

2. See, e.g., Schüssler Fiorenza (1995); Cole and Taussig (2004); Pears (2004).

3. J. D. Crossan believes that the notion of divine Wisdom personified as Sophia was the heart of the "Q" gospel, which may lie behind this Matthean text (1999: 502).

4. Aristophanes' famous comedy *Lysistrata* describes how the twenty-year Peloponnesian War concluded in six days when the women of Athens refused to have sex with their husbands until hostilities ceased! A dramatic testimony to the ancient tradition of women as community peacemakers can be seen in how the entire Lenape clan of the Delaware Valley was appointed by the Iroquois Confederacy to play the role of mediators/peacemakers in tribal conflicts, and collectively are referred to as "women." The account in the Lenape sacred story, the Walam Olum, goes thus: "It is not well that all nations should war; for that will finally bring about the destruction of the Indians. We have thought of a means to prevent this before it is too late. Let one nation be the Woman. We will place her in the middle, and the war nations shall be the Men and dwell around her. No one shall harm the Woman . . . The Woman shall not go to war, but do her best to keep the peace. When the Men around her fight one another, and the strife waxes hot, the Woman will have the power to say, 'You Men! Why do you strike one another? Remember that your wives and children will perish if you do not cease. Will you perish from the face of the earth? Then

from nineteenth-century abolitionist Harriet Tubman to twentieth-century United Farm Workers cofounder Dolores Huerta;[5] from famous civil rights heroine Rosa Parks to forgotten movement martyr Viola Liuzzo;[6] and from Presbyterian advocate for lesbian and gay rights Janie Spahr to recent martyr and Brazilian forest defender Sister Dorothy Stang.[7]

Women's stories have, of course, long been hidden or secondary in the dominant culture to the "heroic feats" (in war and peace) of men.[8] Thus we believe it is important to underline the restorative justice and peacemaking work of women, and this chapter offers the testimony of two who are beloved mentors to us. In their insistence upon speaking truth to power, Liz McAlister and Murphy Davis embody both the prophetic Sophia of Proverbs and the peacemaking Sophia of Ephesians.

One more text comes to mind to describe the witness of these friends— John the Revelator's extraordinary double vision of a woman struggling to protect life in the face of a Beast who threatens incalculable violence:

> A great portent appeared in heaven: a woman clothed with the sun, with the moon under her feet, and on her head a crown of twelve stars. She was pregnant and was crying out in birth pangs, in the agony of giving birth. Then another portent appeared in heaven: a

---

the Men shall listen to the Woman and obey her" (Brinton and Rafinesque, 1885: 110f.). Late nineteenth-century anthropologist Daniel Brinton, from whom this account comes, also notes the skepticism with which European historians apprehended this peacemaking tradition: "Gen Harrison dismisses it as 'impossible'; Albert Gallatin says, 'It is too incredible to require serious discussion'; Mr Hale characterizes it as 'preposterous'; and Bishop de Schweinitz as 'fabulous and absurd'" (1885: 112). Indeed! For overviews of women and peacemaking in the last two centuries, see McAllister (1982); Pierson (1987); Marshall (2008).

5. On Tubman, see Larson (2004); on Huerta, see Worth (2006).

6. In March of 1965, Viola Gregg Liuzzo, a white mother from Detroit, watched on television as State troopers and sheriffs with nightsticks, tear gas and whips attacked the Selma to Montgomery march on Selma's Edmund Pettus Bridge. One hundred marchers were injured on what became known as "Bloody Sunday." Liuzzo was so moved that she drove down to Alabama to join the march into Montgomery. Afterwards, as she was driving marchers back to Selma, she was shot and killed by Klansmen in a passing car. See Stanton (2000).

7. On Janie Spahr's work, see www.spahr.com/revjanie/ and www.tamfs.org. On Sr. Dorothy Stang see Murphy (2007); www.sndohio.org/dotstang.htm.

8. In 2005, a thousand women from more than 150 countries were jointly nominated for the Nobel Peace Prize. The goal was to make visible women's efforts to counter injustice, discrimination, oppression, and violence in the pursuit of peace. The number 1000 was chosen to symbolize the vast numbers of women in the world leading the work for human security and a livable and just future. The nomination sought to accentuate the reality of peacemaking as a collective, collaborative, restorative course of action, and to challenge the idea that peace is made by one or two individuals. See www.1000peacewomen.org.

great red dragon. . . . Then the dragon stood before the woman who was about to bear a child, so that he might devour her child as soon as it was born. And she gave birth to a son. . . . (Rev 12:1-5)

McAlister and Davis have made "Sophia's choice" to stand hopeful "before the face of the Unspeakable" (as Merton so aptly put it)—nuclear weapons, the death penalty, and dehumanizing poverty.

6A. Elizabeth McAlister of Jonah House

Liz McAlister, demonstration at White House, December 2007.

Photo credit: Jonah House, used with permission

Elizabeth McAlister is a mother to many of us in the contemporary faith-rooted peace movement. While we would describe her as a woman of extraordinary courage and discipleship, she would say she is only following the convictions of her heart and mind. A Roman Catholic nun for more than thirteen years, Liz first gained notoriety in the late 1960s because of her nonviolent resistance to the Vietnam War. She married activist Priest Philip Berrigan, and together they founded Jonah House in the inner city of Baltimore, Maryland. In this context Liz has raised three children, mentored hundreds of young activists, served the urban poor, experimented with urban homesteading, and gone to jail for civil resistance.

Jonah House is a gospel-based community committed to nonviolent resistance that for more than thirty years has been on the forefront of prophetic witness against militarism and the nuclear arms race.[9] Currently, a core of four women live in two houses, and are slowly working to transform an abandoned, overgrown cemetery into vegetable gardens populated by goats, chickens, and llamas. The community holds daily Bible studies, following the hermeneutical circle of action and reflection. (Among other things, Liz is a gifted teacher of both scripture and the history of social change. When she leads women's retreats, Liz encour-

---

9. For more information: www.jonahhouse.org.

ages participants to rescue stories of women in the Bible from patriarchal interpreters, and to realize afresh their vocation as women disciples.) On Sundays neighbors join them for scripture, liturgy, and a potluck. Every Tuesday, people in need from their desperately poor neighborhood come to Jonah House to receive boxes of food, blankets, and clothes.

Jonah House's mission is to name publicly the connection between war-making and poverty. Weekly, they hold a vigil at the Pentagon to speak out against nuclear weapons. Their resistance also takes the form of "Plowshares actions," in which nonviolent activists enter military bases and weapons manufacturing facilities and symbolically damage nuclear components, in order to further the "spirit of disarmament" in the United States. In 1983, Liz took part in a Plowshares action at Griffiss Air Force Base, which resulted in a three-year prison sentence. We interviewed Liz on May 21, 2006.

i. From Dissent to Resistance

Responding to a call that came from prayer, Liz decided to enter the convent at age nineteen.

> As a young woman I had an urgent sense that my life needed to be about more. Growing up in the late 1950s, the role models before me were wife and mother, and what women did outside of those traditional vocations was very limited. I grew up in a Catholic household, and although it was a stretch for my parents financially, it was very important to them that I receive a Catholic education. Unfortunately, we did not get the *Catholic Worker* newspaper in my house; in my search for more, exposure to that would have changed things radically for me.[10]

Liz believed that through the religious community she could get the exposure and influence she needed to step deeper into her vocation.

> During my two years in the Novitiate and the following year in the House of Studies, a great deal of time was devoted to silence, study of scripture, and prayer. The outcomes for me were personal growth and a radical shift in my view of the world. When I began looking at news reports again, I had a distinct lens that I was looking through. As I read about U.S. advisors in Vietnam, it was immediately offensive to my new worldview. Morally it was clearly wrong to

---

10. For more information on the Catholic Worker movement, see chapter 4, n. 8.

me that we were carrying on our anticommunist war at the expense
of the people of Vietnam and Indochina. At that time, this was not
a political decision for me, it was a moral issue. Political education
followed.

After graduating from university, Liz was assigned by her religious
order to teach at Marymount College in Tarrytown, New York. One
course she taught was Principles of Art Criticism, a senior seminar class
where they studied different authors.

The students and I agreed the following questions would serve as
ground rules for our discussion, "What is the author saying? What
do I think about their theory, what makes sense and what doesn't?
What can be useful to me in standing before works of art?" We were
studying art philosopher Susanne Langer's theory about how symbolic form points beyond itself to something else (see Langer, 1957).
One student stood up and gave a wonderful summary of the key elements of Langer's idea. She then skipped all the other ground rules
we had so conscientiously agreed upon, put her hands on her hips
and said, "Well if you believe that about art, then you would support
what David Miller just did!"
   David Miller was the first to burn his draft card publicly after
it was made a felony offense by Congress. I responded, "You have
made a wonderful leap from art to life. David Miller's action was
an ideal act of symbolic form as Susanne Langer would define it.
And as a matter of fact, I do support what he did." The student in
turn defended our presence in Vietnam, which shocked me because
I thought everyone had outgrown that view, like I had. I had never
had a conversation like that, and I struggled to come to a bit of clarity
with the students. The next week I learned that I was a "pacifist"!

Liz smiles as she relates the story about the unfolding struggles in her
religious order and college community.

I needed to find out what being labeled a "pacifist" meant. Through
research I found that there indeed were members of my religious
order who were against the Vietnam War. One sister suggested
books to read, and she would encourage me to sign out a car so we
could go together to antiwar meetings in New York City. I remember one meeting in particular where I felt I was watching a tennis
match as the heated discussion went back and forth about how we
could move from dissent to resistance. It was a hairy time. The college community was as divided as the whole culture. Worship was

like a battleground, as people couched their positions for or against the war in prayers. It was a nightmare in that sense, but somehow I discovered who I could talk to and who I couldn't as I tried to grow in my newfound understanding.

Liz and others from her religious order who were against the war began providing support to draft resisters taking sanctuary in churches. They also supported the resistance activities of the Catholic Worker: blockades at induction centers, fasts of reconciliation, and silent vigils. And they participated in major marches.

After big actions in New York City, we would gather at our sister college, Marymount Manhattan, to debrief together. These sessions were informal, but upon reflection, what we did without being aware of it was create community. Everyone who took part in these debriefings remained, throughout their lives, involved in nonviolence and resistance. This was during a time when psychologists were telling us that people in the antiwar movement would only stay involved for six months. This was not true for people who, through these gatherings, had support.

At that time, I assumed that everyone had somewhere to go to after actions. But the tragedy is that most people went to their homes, campuses, or jobs where they were criticized for what they were doing. There was no strengthening of their position and no community where they could talk about these struggles. It was such a gift to those of us who had it and, as a result, when the phone call came that we were needed at another action, we would go. We could not *not* go.

In the summer of 1967, Josephite priest Philip Berrigan was at the center of the resistance movement in New York City.[11] He was writing about the problem that draft resisters were being jailed, but priests and nuns could go visit them in prison and then be free to leave. Phil was acutely aware that those in the religious community who were encouraging people to resist were not taking the same risks.

On October 17, 1967, after doing a variety of protests at military bases and talking with generals at the Pentagon, Phil and three others did the first of what became a series of daring break-ins. They entered the Baltimore Selective Service office and poured their own

---

11. For background on the events alluded to here, see P. Berrigan and Wilcox (1996) and Polner and O'Grady (1997).

blood on draft files. The idea for this action had come from a Quaker clan that had a long history of resistance to this nation's wars. Early on in the Vietnam War, this family collected its fecal material in a bucket. The father then went to a draft board and poured the bucket on 1-A draft records—an action coined as "the movements that began a movement." Phil decided to use blood instead, which ironically many people found even more repulsive.

The following day, I heard an announcement on the radio about some unnamed persons who had poured blood on draft files. The reporter's tone was utterly dismissive, but because of my art background studying symbolic forms, I wanted to know why these people did this. When I learned that it was Phil and others, I was deeply grateful. Some of us from my religious community went to the trial of the "Baltimore Four," where I learned a great deal.[12]

Shortly afterwards, I got a call from George Mische to meet in New York City. George told the five of us gathered that he and others were making plans to do a similar action. He pointed his finger at each of us and said, "What about you?" I looked behind me, thinking he couldn't be pointing at me! I did not participate in what became the Catonsville Nine action. But in time I began to understand that conversation, particularly in studying the book of Revelation: "I will give you a white stone on which your name is written and no one knows except the one who receives it" (Rev 2:17). This is a "finger pointing," an invitation to a new identity.

On May 17, 1968, George Mische, Phil and Daniel Berrigan, and six others walked into the selective service office in Catonsville, Maryland, seized some draft files and carried them out into the parking lot. There they burned the files with a homemade version of napalm, the jellied gasoline that was being used to such deadly effect in Vietnam. Daniel Berrigan famously said in the group's statement afterward, "Our apologies, good friends, for the fracture of good order, the burning of paper instead of children."[13]

Such actions were too new for me. When I sat down with a close friend to try to explain what the action was and why I was considering participating in it, I could only explain in borrowed phrases. I didn't yet have my own words. It takes nine months for a pregnant

12. See also the history site for war resistance in Maryland: http://mdvietnamera.org/
13. For more on the Catonsville Nine action and the ensuing trial, each of which represented watershed moments in American public religious and political theater, see D. Berrigan (2004).

woman to nurture a child and I couldn't do that preparation in a couple of weeks.

The seed was planted, however, and Liz later took part in a draft board action in Wilmington, Delaware, in which she and other activists took files and wrote each of the young men to give them another chance to sign or not sign up for the military. On the same night, another group did a similar action at a draft board in Dover, Maryland. In all there were over a hundred draft board actions around the country, making a dramatic impact on the ability of the Selective Service System to function.[14]

ii. Plowshares Actions as Public Liturgy

After Liz and Phil were married, they founded Jonah House. Liz recognized the power of community early on, and knew that if they were going to continue in their resistance, they needed to support and encourage one another. The community's purpose was to continue to deepen their resistance to the war in Vietnam. In 1973, the war was still raging, but there were fewer headlines, as the general public grew weary of it. Liz and Phil's intent was to keep the war and its violence in front of the public through continued resistance.

In April 1975, the U.S. military abandoned its efforts in Vietnam. The community's attention turned toward an even deeper level of state violence: nuclear weapons and policy. Members of Jonah House recognized that strategic weapons systems had become ever more sophisticated, and began researching them in order to expand strategies for resistance.

We learned about the overt change of nuclear policy from Mutual Assured Destruction to Flexible and Strategic Targeting Options. This change involved two major things. One was the retargeting of all U.S. missiles away from Soviet cities to Soviet weapons and their storage, bunkers, fields, and industry. The other was the development of the disarming first strike capability that allowed us to target our missiles so accurately that we could take out an opponent's missiles before they were launched. We felt this change of policy made nuclear war more imminent, so we began to educate ourselves about those ramifications. It also forced us to recognize what our govern-

---

14. For a general history and analysis of draft resistance during this period, see Foley (2003).

ment had been doing while we were focused on the Vietnam War, which was an eye opener.[15]

We spent years researching nuclear weapons bases and manufacturers. The question became, "How do we resist this new strategy?" Obviously we can't readily get into the nuclear planners' offices and destroy their records. So we began a regular presence at the White House and the Pentagon, which continues to this day.

In 1980, members of Jonah House and the Atlantic Life Community, a wider circle of East Coast peace colleagues, began exploring ideas of how to "render these weapons unusable." In September of that year, a group including Dan and Phil Berrigan inaugurated the Plowshares movement, entering a General Electric plant at King of Prussia, Pennsylvania, and hammering on Mark 12A nuclear warhead nosecones.[16] This remarkable new expression of what Bill Wylie Kellermann rightly calls "public liturgy" was inspired by Isaiah 2:4, "They shall beat swords into plowshares and their spears into pruning hooks; nation shall not lift up sword against nation, nor shall they learn war any more."[17] With this action having garnered significant attention, Jonah House looked at doing another one.

I believed that the same people involved in the first action should not do the next one. There might be many others who would want to be involved in this kind of nonviolent resistance, so the organizing began. I also wondered about the possibility of whether I, now a mother of three young children, should participate.

On Thanksgiving Day, 1983, Liz and six other women and men entered Griffiss Air Force Base in Rome, New York.[18] Art Laffin, in his chronicle of the Plowshares movement, describes the action:

---

15. For a succinct and compelling analysis of U.S. first strike nuclear capacity, see Aldridge (1989).

16. See Myers (1987). The eight were subsequently arrested and tried by a jury, convicted, and sentenced to prison terms ranging from one and a half to ten years. After a series of appeals lasting ten years, they were resentenced to time served—from several days to seventeen and a half months. For a chronology of Plowshares actions, see Laffin (2003; also at www.craftech.com/~dcpledge/brandywine/plow/webpages/webintro2.htm); Nepstad (2008).

17. See also Micah 4:3. For a theological and political analysis of public liturgy and symbolic direct action, see Kellermann (1991).

18. The other participants were: Jackie Allen, a teacher from Hartford, Connecticut; Clare Grady, an artist from Ithaca, New York; Kathleen Rumpf, a Catholic Worker from Marlboro, New York; Dean Hammer, a veteran of the Plowshares Eight action three years

They hammered and poured blood on a B-52 bomber that had been converted to carry cruise missiles, as well as on B-52 engines. They also left at the site of their witness a written indictment of Griffiss Air Force Base and the U.S. Government pointing to the war crimes of preparing for nuclear war and depicting how the new state religion of "nuclearism" denies constitutional rights and punishes acts of conscience. Unnoticed for several hours, they finally approached security guards and were arrested. . . . They were acquitted by a jury of sabotage, but they were convicted of conspiracy and destruction of government property. They received prison sentences ranging from two to three years. Their appeal was denied in federal court in March 1985. (2003: 51)

While the five previous Plowshares actions had all resulted in state charges, the seven Griffiss defendants were the first to receive a federal indictment. Liz was sentenced to three years in prison.

I could not have done this action unless I felt under the mandate of scripture to beat swords into plowshares, nor without the discernment and support from Phil and others at Jonah House. Entering the Air Force base and hammering on a B-52 bomber was a momentous thing to do, and yet I had to do something against this death system.

The focus of our action was to slow down the first strike capability. Other Plowshares actions had focused on the Trident Submarine and its missiles, the Mark 12-A and so forth. We selected the B-52 at Griffiss Air Force Base because it was retrofitted to be the carrier for air launch cruise missiles, weapons which fly low to avoid radar detection and seek out hardened targets. We damaged the plane, its engines and refuelers, and other accompanying aircraft, all of which were tied up in the subsequent investigations, and therefore inoperable for several months. So we did slow the system down a little bit.

Within the wider peace movement there is heated debate about direct actions that involves property destruction. Plowshares witnesses have thus been very controversial because of the risks involved, their explicitly religious rationale, and their tactical goal to symbolically damage military hardware.

Plowshares actions might not be *the* way, but they are *a* way of stating very clearly, "These weapons have no right to exist." We do these

---

earlier; Vern Rossman, a minister and grandfather from Boston; and Karl Smith, a member of Jonah House.

nonviolent actions knowing the risk to our own freedom and to our lives when we enter "deadly force" areas. We act with our sisters and brothers in a powerful community, but there are risks for our community and for our children. I did this action with three small children at home; our youngest Kate was two and half years old. I served two years in prison.[19]

Liz is deeply concerned for her children and others around the world, since the young are most adversely affected by war. Her commitment to nonviolent resistance has infused all three of her children. As adults each is involved in unique expressions of peace and justice work.

Liz believes all disciples are called to work toward a spiritual climate of disarmament.

We aim to release an unequivocal "spirit of disarmament" through our actions. We bring this spirit into the courtroom where, rather than trying to get out of a sentence, we try to explain why we did the action. While we are in prison serving our sentences, we continue to defend our actions. We stand by what we have done, and believe it brings hope.

The action, the trials, and serving time all provide a platform to organize locally, nationally, and internationally. We do not pretend that our small communities can destroy all of these weapons. The death system will not be disarmed until the spiritual climate of this nation turns and becomes convinced that we should not be building these weapons. We cannot calculate the power that goes out from these actions, or what the results will be. But we hope our actions will lead to a climate of disarmament.

U.S. foreign policy is based on domination and violence. We use our weapons to bully the rest of the world. This is empire, and people of conscience cannot accept the violence that impoverishes the majority in order to provide wealth for the few. Weapons technology gets ever more sophisticated and increasingly removed from anything human. We all need to see ourselves as instruments of nonviolent resistance, to keep the spirit of disarmament alive. Disarming the world requires our hearts to be disarmed.

Since the first Plowshares action, there have been some eighty-five similar witnesses all over the world.[20] Liz cautions about trying to measure their effectiveness, and suggests instead that we focus on living faithfully.

---

19. Some of Liz's prison reflections are found in Berrigan and McAlister (1989).
20. In a witness dear to Liz's heart and for which she played an enormous support

We don't know what effectiveness really means; and whose value system are we using trying to calculate it? People have been very critical because of this. Our friend Sam Day, who was for many years the managing editor of *The Progressive* magazine, once collected all of the data on acts of nuclear resistance, and summarized all the ways these actions are effective. While that was a gift to us, we do not pin our hopes on it. It is best to avoid this kind of scorekeeping, because it doesn't make us more human or more loving. We live in a culture of measurements, calculations, and five-year plans, but I don't believe they help us. I believe if we are faithful, the results will take care of themselves.

In 1969, when we did the draft board actions, I had no way of knowing how many of those men that we wrote to actually chose not to go into the military. And in a sense it is not ours to know. But recently I was taking my nephew's son to the airport, and walked him out to the gate because he was underage. Together we were a McAlister and a Berrigan. The man at the ticket counter said, "Now, those are familiar names. Years ago, I was designated a 1-A out of Catonsville. In destroying my draft record, you saved my life!" Experiences such as that happen just often enough to give me light and hope to go on.

6B. Murphy Davis of the Open Door Community

Thirty years ago, Liz's husband Phil wrote: "The Holy Spirit reminds us that until we name the Beast, expose its lies and curb, however modestly,

---

role, Jonah House community members Ardeth Platte and Carol Gilbert, together with Jackie Hudson—all Dominican Sisters in their sixties—did a Plowshares action on October 6, 2003, the anniversary of the bombing of Afghanistan. The nuns entered a Minute Man III silo N-8 near Greeley, Colorado, dressed in white mop-up suits, with "Citizens Weapons Inspection Team" printed on the back and "Disarmament Specialists" on the front. They cut the chain securing the gates surrounding the silo, and proceeded to pour their blood in the form of a cross six times on the 110-ton silo lid and on the tracks that carry the lid to the firing position. In a ritual of prayer and symbolic disarmament, they then used household hammers on the silo and the tracks. The three nuns were arrested, jailed, charged, and convicted of obstructing the national defense and destruction of government property, felonies that carry up to thirty years in federal prison. The government pressed sabotage charges, and the three sisters were convicted, receiving sentences of thirty to forty-one months. Their story is told in a documentary produced by Brenda Truelson Fox entitled *Conviction* (Zero to Sixty Productions, 2006), which explores the action, and the roles of religion in politics, of nuclear weapons in national defense, and of international law in the federal courts.

Murphy Davis, detail from Americans Who Tell the Truth Portrait Series, by Robert Shetterly.

Photo: www.americanswhotellthe truth.org, used with permission

its destructiveness, it names us, defines us, enslaves us as accomplices in its colossal crimes" (P. Berrigan, 1978: i). The idolatry of the Bomb represents the ultimate shadow of death, under which we all dwell. Murphy Davis, meanwhile, has been working to confront another face of the Unspeakable: the death penalty and the cold shadow it casts over the life of the poor.

Murphy is a tireless advocate for the poorest of America: those on the streets and on death row. She and her husband, Eduard Loring, are Presbyterian ministers who work intently on the related issues of homelessness, prison, poverty, class, and racial segregation. In 1981, they founded The Open Door Community (ODC), in an old apartment building near downtown Atlanta where Christians struggle with the difficult terrain of working and living together across race, class, and gender lines.[21] Some of the residents were once homeless or in prison, while others are ministers, students, or lawyers. The ODC daily offers the basic necessities of food, clothing, showers, toilets, telephone use, and shelter to the homeless of Atlanta. Murphy also founded Southern Prison Ministry, which raises critical awareness of the criminal justice system and provides advocacy and hope for those caught in it.

Murphy is a powerful preacher and teacher who brings rigorous analysis together with compelling stories of her accompaniment work. In 1995, she was diagnosed with an often fatal form of cancer. After each of three rounds of intensive surgery and treatments, her cancer has gone into remission; at this writing, she is in the midst of a fourth round. Her friends on Georgia's death row and on the streets of Atlanta storm heaven with prayers for this beloved woman, who is to them an angel, steadfast in her solidarity and companionship. Elaine interviewed Murphy on May 23, 2006.

---

21. For more information see: www.opendoorcommunity.org. For a history of and reflections from the community's life, see volumes edited by Gathje (1991, 2002, 2006).

i. Learning from the Persistent Widow

Murphy grew up in the South in the 1950s, and there came to conscious-ness about race, class, and prisons.

> From an early age I witnessed chain gangs as a version of slavery—black men in striped suits, and a white man with a rifle—and it nagged at me. We lived in a very conservative area of North Car-olina—a mean place in many ways, and completely locked down racially. But my parents were opposed to any kind of violent retribu-tion, and I am very thankful for the context they set. I knew as a child the death penalty was abhorrent and wrong. The civil rights movement was well afoot by the time I was in high school. From a young age I was called a "n-i-g-g-e-r lover," accused of being a race traitor. Although I had friends and a social life, I had a clear sense of standing outside of the dominant culture.

Murphy spent her young adult years at Mary Baldwin College, a women's school nestled in Virginia's Shenandoah Valley. In 1967, she got involved in the black community there, joining the local NAACP and serving as organist in a black Methodist church.

> Dr. King's death was a turning point for me. I knew I had to some-how live an interracial life. But at that point, I had no idea how dif-ficult that would be and the relentless effort it takes to break down the barriers. During the summer of 1969, when I was studying at the University of Denver, I took an abnormal psychology course with a wonderful professor, Bernard Spilka. One day in class he announced, "I meet with a group of Chicano men in the Colorado State prison, and I am going there this Wednesday night. If any one in the class wants to go, you can come." I knew immediately that I would go, because I wanted to experience it and hear their stories.
>
> Chicanos were the majority of that prison population, and the group was meeting to address violence in the prison. They formed this group called the Latin American Development Society to help each other pull away from the automatic response of fighting, which is part of the everyday degradation of a captive population. At my first meeting a group of men got me in a corner and "work-shopped" me, as they say in civil rights. I got an earful. The prison was only five years beyond regular use of the bullwhip, and it curled my teeth to hear their stories. At that moment, it became clear to me that I was going to do something related to this struggle.

Murphy returned to Mary Baldwin to finish her last year, far removed from the Colorado State Penitentiary. But her experience had changed her, and after graduation she moved to Atlanta. She explored law school, but soon realized she wanted to go to Seminary, and in 1971 began studies at Columbia Theological Seminary.

I was deeply involved in the women's movement and antiwar and civil rights work. To keep my focus on prison, I volunteered weekly at the Fulton County Children's Detention Center. When I finished Seminary, I was accepted to do a PhD at Emory University with a full fellowship in church history. I was interested in nineteeth-century women's history and black history, because of the intersection of chivalry and slavery. How did the role of women and the place of slavery shape each other? But none of the professors understood my idea. There were no women on faculty at Columbia and no women's studies courses in the entire university! I finally realized that the school expected me to do the required course work full time, and pursue my other interests in whatever time I might have left over—which was impossible. It was a bad match for me and I was completely frustrated.

In the summer of 1976, the Georgia death penalty law, which had been struck down by the U.S. Supreme Court in 1972, then rewritten by Governor Jimmy Carter in 1973, was upheld by the Court in *Gregg v. Georgia*.[22] She had just finished her first year in the PhD program, and gotten married to fellow Presbyterian minister Eduard Loring.

Ed was involved in a small, ad hoc group called "Georgia Christians against the Death Penalty," so I began attending their meetings. When I heard several mothers of men on death row speak about their lives and struggles, about the injustice and sorrow they bore, and about what it was like to have a son sentenced to die, I felt called out.

---

22. The death penalty is primarily an issue of state rather than federal law. Of the fifty states, thirty-eight currently have the death penalty. At the federal level, capital punishment has rarely been used over the past forty years; the most notorious execution was of Timothy McVeigh, one of the perpetrators of the 1995 bombing of the Federal Building in Oklahoma City. The Georgia death penalty law was struck in *Furman v. Georgia*, because of inconsistency in its application. *Gregg v. Georgia* looked at whether the imposition of the sentence of death for murder violated the Eighth and Fourteenth Amendments as cruel and unusual punishment. In a 7-to-2 decision, the Supreme Court held that the death penalty did not violate these amendments under all circumstances, and could be used "carefully and judiciously." It was seven years before Georgia executed someone.

The prison where their sons were held allowed noncontact visitation only (i.e., with thick wire-mesh screens between them), and every week after visiting, these women would go to the warden's office and cry. Week after week, they begged to be able to hug and comfort their sons. The warden was a very hard man, but he got so tired of women blubbering all over his office that he granted contact visits! It made me think of the persistent widow and the callous judge in Luke 18:2-5. One woman in particular, Viva Lamb, was a hair dresser with not much education, but she took up her role as leader and changed minds and hearts by telling her story in her lovely Arkansas twang. Like Luke's widow, she was so powerless, yet accomplished what no one else could.

Listening to and learning from Viva, Murphy knew she would have to make a big change. She had not forgotten the prisoners at Colorado State Penitentiary, who had taken time to share their stories.

Some weeks later, at 2 A.M., I shut my textbook and said, "Ed, I am not doing this anymore. I've got to do something real!" I got a job shortly thereafter with the Southern Coalition on Jail and Prisons, coordinating a national demonstration in Atlanta against the death penalty on Easter weekend, 1977. Miraculously, I walked out of graduate school and straight to the center of the movement.

Murphy successfully brought together leadership of the American Civil Liberties Union, Amnesty International, civil rights movement, state coalitions, and religious groups to protest the death penalty.

We turned out three thousand people for a march and rally in Atlanta. Journalist Tom Wicker and former U.S. attorney general Ramsey Clark were there, as were many church leaders, two men who had been exonerated and freed from death row in Florida, mothers of men on death row—all of whom offered very powerful testimony.

Soon after, Murphy set up Southern Prison Ministry (SPM) to work specifically with folks on death row and women in prison. SPM members campaign against the death penalty by exposing incompetence, racism, and political maneuvering in the criminal justice system. They also call for alternatives to prisons through vigils, protests, marches, and lobbying at the state legislature. Members visit and correspond with people on death row, conduct research and education, and provide opportunities for college students and others to learn about prisons. Each month SPM transports up to a hundred family and friends who cannot afford the journey from Atlanta to Hardwick Prison to visit their incarcerated loved ones.

Murphy herself has made innumerable visits to death row prisoners, befriending hundreds, and immersing herself in the struggle to abolish the death penalty. The 1972 *Furman v. Georgia* decision had struck down the death penalty because it was so overwhelmingly racially discriminatory. The new capital punishment statute in Georgia was similarly tested in 1987 at the Supreme Court in *McCleskey v. Kemp.*

Warren McCleskey was one of our dearest friends on death row. His lawyers drew on the work of scholars David Baldus, Charles Pulaski, and George Woodworth (1990), who did incredible statistical analysis of all murder cases in Georgia from 1973 to 1978. They indicated that a different sort of discrimination was emerging: people who received the death penalty had killed a "valued member" of society (which in the U.S. almost always means a white person). They showed that if someone killed a white person in Georgia, they were four times more likely to receive a death sentence than if they had killed a nonwhite person. If a black person killed a white person, they were ten times more likely to receive the death penalty. Their study proved *again* that the death penalty is completely discriminatory and should be struck down.

In a long-awaited decision, the Supreme Court ruled 5-to-4 that this shameful pattern made no difference, and upheld Georgia's death penalty. The Court argued that the accused had to prove that racial prejudice *animated* his judge, his prosecutor or his jury.

Justice Lewis Powell was the swing vote, and went with the majority to uphold the Georgia death penalty law. In the decision he wrote, "To overturn the Georgia death penalty law would be to potentially dismantle the criminal justice system in the U.S." I believe that Powell understood that racial discrimination in exercising death penalty law is essential to the character of the criminal control system in the U.S. Our friend Warren McCleskey was executed in September 1991.

That same year, Justice Powell retired. In his biography, Powell indicated that in retrospect, he would change his vote in the McCleskey case: "I have come to think that capital punishment should be abolished" (Jeffries, 2001: 451f.).

Former U.S. attorney general Ramsey Clark named the nature of this system in his 1970 book *Crime in America: Observations on Its Nature,*

Causes, Prevention, and Control, concluding: "Our history shows that the death penalty has been unjustly imposed, innocents have been killed by the state, effective rehabilitation has been impaired, judicial administration has suffered. It is the poor, the sick, the ignorant, the powerless, and the hated who are executed" (1970: 330). Murphy has countless stories such as the following that illustrate Clark's indictment.

> Lois, a woman I know who is the mother of a man on death row, says, "My son, who is a paranoid schizophrenic, was turned out of a mental hospital because our health insurance ran out. They knew he wasn't well but the money was gone so his treatment was over. His condition got worse and he killed someone. Now the state is spending four million dollars to try to kill him. There's all this money to kill him but there was none to help him. What kind of sense does that make?" (in Gathje, 2002: 147)

ii. Poverty and Prisons: Opposite Ends of the Same System

Murphy has done extensive research on the experience of incarceration, the rapid growth of the prison industrial complex, and the disturbing relationship between prison expansion and the decline of affordable housing. She focuses her work on the opposite ends of the criminal justice system—crime and homelessness—in order to explain how the two are inextricably linked.

> Most offenses that homeless folks are arrested for are actually status crimes, which have to do with poverty, such as public urination or trespass. Trespass is often about a homeless person trying to sleep in an abandoned car or building, or on the edge of someone's property. Last summer, we lost a long-standing struggle when the City Council finally bowed to the will of the elite white business community. For more than twenty years, this group has tried to exclude from downtown Atlanta poor, black men who "scare" white people. One of their legal tools is arrest for public urination—several hundred people every month. If downtown Atlanta smells like urine and feces, wouldn't a logical response be to have public toilets? Since 1983, we have been fighting for public toilets, and the main opposition has come from these business folk. It is obvious that the issue is not public urination; it is having laws to get homeless people out of the way.
>
> Sometimes folks are arrested for public indecency. This is a whole different level of humiliation that the poor are subjected to simply

because they need to relieve themselves. Humiliation is part of the system against the very poor. We have people in our home at the Open Door on a daily basis who are in and out of jail for crimes that are on the books simply to control the poor.

On the other end of the spectrum, we have the death penalty, which is also about control. If the government is legally allowed to kill its own citizens, especially folks who we define as "other," or "less than," it can justify most anything. People become objects to be moved around, caged, punished. A person can be moved off a park bench, or onto a gurney, strapped down and killed. Humiliation is also what death row is about. The only thing that people know about you is what you did or allegedly did in one moment of your life. You are completely defined by that one moment. I ask groups: "Think about the worst thing you have ever done in your life, the thing you do *not* want others to know. What if that was the *only* thing people knew about you?" For a lot of us, that thing would not be murder, but it would be ugly. None of us want to be defined by our worst act.

The connection between homeless people and death row is very logical to us. If you are homeless you are dying, because you don't have the most basic necessities to stay alive—food, shelter, health care, a bed, a toilet. Homelessness is a nonjudicial confinement where you are "sentenced" to a death of poverty and deprivation.

Murphy's years of advocacy and her incisive analysis have yielded a frightening picture of the current criminal justice system. She does not believe this system provides justice for victims, offenders, or their families; rather, she sees its primary function as control.

The system is about controlling surplus populations and in most places in the U.S. this means primarily nonwhite and poor people. In the South it means black folks and, increasingly, Latinos. We need to be clear here, though many in the system resist this: we are putting people—including children—in cages, and practicing violent retribution.

For example, the increasing rate of female incarceration is decimating black and Latino families and communities. While there are still far fewer women in prison then men, the rate of increase over the last twelve to fifteen years has been much faster. This is largely due to the drug war. Five years ago, legislation mandated that penalties for possession or sale of crack cocaine would be significantly greater than those for powder cocaine. Three years ago evidence was brought to Congress showing that black people were receiving disproportionately long sentences for possessing crack cocaine, while white people using or dealing powder cocaine got short sentences or probation. It was irrefutable evidence of a racially discriminatory law, but Congress declined to do anything about it.[23]

When I first began working on these issues in the 1970s, the Federal Bureau of Prisons projected their need for new construction on the basis of unemployment statistics. Now the projections are on the basis of the disjointed and decimated lives of black children. They are looking at the lives of seven-year-old black children to predict how many prison beds they will need. These children never have a chance; they are being groomed for prison life.

To understand this, Murphy contends, we need to look at the struggle over the Thirteenth Amendment to the Constitution soon after the Civil War.

It was a pitched battle between forces led by Senator Charles Sumner of Massachusetts, who was an abolitionist, and the allies of the Southern Planter class. Sumner and his allies wanted the Thirteenth Amendment to read "Neither slavery nor involuntary servitude . . ." The Southern Planters wanted it to read "Neither slavery nor involuntary servitude *except* as punishment for a crime of which the person is duly convicted."

The Southern position prevailed. Although the Thirteenth Amendment, adopted on December 6, 1865, officially abolished slavery, those convicted of a crime could nevertheless be subject to involuntary servitude.

As a result, Murphy maintains, the system continues to dilute the rights of prisoners.

In the South, a whole set of vagrancy laws grew up called the "black codes." These made it possible for the police and other powers to have complete discretion in the arrest, trial, and conviction of black people. This, in turn, allowed the reenslavement of work forces on plantations and railroads, in turpentine and lumber mills, etc. Many of the white elites who held power and who helped to force the end of Reconstruction had businesses leasing convicts.

Today, the Thirteenth Amendment provides the legal foundation

---

23. For more analysis on this issue see Miller (1997), who points out that "the war on drugs, begun in the Reagan Administration and presently continuing unabated, has resulted in an explosion in the American prison population . . . accounted for by a severely disproportionate number of African American males."

for penal slavery. People in prison are, by law, slaves of the state; there is very little accountability for how prisoners are treated. If a prison guard tells a prisoner to work and they refuse, the prisoner can be put in solitary confinement or suffer other disciplinary tactics. Prisoners make airline reservations, lingerie for Victoria's Secret, conduct tele-marketing for AT&T, and sell computer parts—often for no wage or for just a few cents an hour. This forced labor is benefiting corporations and undercutting the free labor market!

Fortunately, there have been some rights defined by legislation and court decisions that recognize that prisoners aren't entirely non-persons. But we have almost destroyed Habeas Corpus, which has been basic to the English and American systems for centuries.[24] "The Anti-Terrorism and Effected Death Penalty Act" passed after the Oklahoma City bombing, and the Patriot Act which came in the wake of 9/11, have all tremendously altered Habeas Corpus so that the rights of the accused are more diminished today then they ever have been in the American legal system!

Things have gone so far that actual fact of innocence will not necessarily save a person from being executed. The U.S. Supreme Court said in the 1982 appeal of Roger Coleman of Virginia that "factual innocence is not enough to stop an execution. If procedurally the case is sound, we are choosing to ignore factual innocence."[25] Most people do not pay much attention to the direction and decisions of the Supreme Court, because "criminals" do not have a constituency. But when Habeas Corpus is torn apart, it affects all of us.

iii. Solidarity with the Executed

For all her prophetic advocacy, the heart of Murphy's work is pastoral: visiting prisoners on death row, listening to their stories, and advocating for them.

Biblical faith calls for solidarity with "the least." But the most difficult case is the guilty least, the obnoxious least. We believe these folks have created their own mess and don't want to recognize that

---

24. Inherited from fourteenth-century English Common Law, the Habeas Corpus Act was formalized in the United States in 1679, and became an inalienable right in the Bill of Rights. It is the primary means whereby an individual who is incarcerated can challenge the lawfulness of that detention.

25. Similarly, when a prisoner condemned to death petitioned a Virginia Circuit Court to review new evidence on his behalf, then attorney general Mary Sue Terry argued: "Evidence of innocence is irrelevant" (see www.cstone.net/~vadp/21day.htm).

we have common interests with people who have committed terrible crimes. Three of our friends from Georgia's death row have recently been released—none of whom were innocent. It is easy for people to feel that the innocent should get out; but solidarity with the guilty is where our faith is really tested.

The loss of her friends on death row hits her hard. Murphy relates her first journey through that fire in Advent of 1983. Georgia's first execution under the new statute was John Eldon Smith, a fifty-four-year-old white man whom Murphy had visited for four years.

The days following the killing found our community about the tasks of burial and comforting Smitty's family . . . One week later we made a feeble effort to pick ourselves up to prepare Christmas dinner for our homeless friends. The temperatures in Atlanta suddenly fell to zero and below . . . Even as we celebrated the Nativity of our Lord, twenty of our homeless sisters and brothers died in the streets and alleyways of our city . . . frozen stiff in dark corners, abandoned cars, vacant buildings. . . . Day and night we cooked hot food and fixed hot coffee and tea to take out onto the streets. We squeezed as many extra bodies into our dining room as the space would bear. . . . Nothing in my background as a white overeducated Christian; nothing in my studies; nothing in my spiritual instruction or pastoral counseling—nothing had prepared me to meet with such utter failure, grief, and suffering (Gathje, 2002: 250)

Murphy writes about losing another good friend on January 9, 1985, and what she learned from him:

Roosevelt Green was . . . one of the most self-aware, politically astute human beings I have ever known. At ten minutes after midnight on that cold winter's night, he walked calmly into the execution chamber and made the following statement: "The night I was arrested and taken into the Monroe County Jail, one of the jailers said to me, 'Boy, the lives of two niggers still ain't enough to make up for one white life.' I didn't believe him on that night. I thought he was wrong. Tonight I know he . . . spoke for this society, which is racist from top to bottom. I will die before you tonight because I am black—and because I was associated with another black man who killed a white woman. But my life will not be enough to satisfy you. You will kill me and still be hungry for revenge. The one thing you cannot do is make me hate you. I will not hate you even though you kill me. I forgive you, for you are blind. I will die with peace in my heart." (Ibid.: 176f.)

Murphy's stories are often hilarious and heartbreaking all at once, such as her account of Jerome Bowden, a developmentally disabled African American man who had grown up in Muscogee County, Georgia, where his mother worked as a maid for the county sheriff.

Jerome and his sister grew up eating surplus commodity food because his mother was not paid a living wage. His whole life was something of a death row even before he got to prison. There he remained for a number of years before he was executed in June 1986. Jerome had a simple, childlike approach to life. . . . I love the time he told us about the Bible study they were having in his cell block, on the Book of Revelation. Jerome wanted to understand Revelation so badly that he kept saying to others, "Look, can't you just break this down for me just a little bit? Can't you explain this thing to me?" Finally, one of his friends drew a chart of Revelation . . .

We went to see Jerome one day, and he was dying laughing. He started to tell us the story of how the guards had come into the cell-block for a shakedown. They threw his stuff all over the floor and looked for contraband and weapons. One guard came across Jerome's chart of Revelation. He was convinced that it was an escape plan! So Jerome's chart was confiscated and taken straightaway to the warden's office, where numerous prison bureaucrats put their heads together over the chart of the Book of Revelation. They tried to fig-ure out how Jerome Bowden was going to escape death row with this chart. And Jerome couldn't stop laughing. But he never got his chart back.

When Jerome's execution date was set, the Georgia Association for Retarded Citizens took his case and began to advocate for him. A stay of execution lasted for several days. During that time the Board of Pardons and Paroles sent an Emory University psychologist to study Jerome and to determine just how retarded he was. The con-clusion drawn by this eminent psychologist was that Jerome Bowden was retarded, but not quite retarded enough to be spared. What an ironic twist that the test the psychologist used asked Jerome to define the word sanctuary. Jerome said, "A place to go and be safe." And it killed him. (Ibid.: 30f.)

Often a person who has been on death row for many years has lost all contact with family and friends—just as familial ties for many homeless people have been broken. If no one claims their bodies, they are made invisible and humiliated in death. Murphy writes about how she and others were able to give a dignified burial to the second person executed under Georgia's 1976 law in July 1984:

> I stood in a field that was surrounded by barbed wire near the town of Jackson, outside a Georgia prison that has become for many of us the representation and the presence of hell itself. About thirty of us stood in a circle, and we held each others' hands and what must have looked like pitiful, flickering little candles. In the dark hours of the early morning we sang hymns.
>
> Out of the darkness came an official procession—the front-office prison men in their suits and ties. They were surrounded and swallowed up by the lights and the television cameras. Then came the official proclamation: Ivon Ray Stanley, a twenty-eight-year-old functionally retarded black man, died calmly in the electric chair at 12:24 A.M. No complications, a nice clean execution. After eight years on death row, Stanley was convicted and sentenced to die by a jury of twelve white, church-going folks of Bainbridge, Georgia, who saw revenge as the proper Christian response to violence.
>
> Ivon Ray Stanley was officially dead. The state had spoken. Then there were tears in that field, sobs and groans: "Jesus, have mercy." The mother, grandmother, the sister-in-law, the friend—each was broken, hurt, defeated. "Jesus, Jesus, have mercy." It was very dark in that field.
>
> The next day, Friday, we stood in another circle. But this time the soil under our feet was free soil; it was sanctuary. We gathered at the edge of a beautiful pasture at the Jubilee Community in Comer, Georgia.[26] We gathered to bury our friend Ivon Ray Stanley. . . . When we seek to serve our Lord in the broken and oppressed and suffering flesh of the poor, then we are called to bury the dead as one more of the acts of mercy. . . . We gathered around the cold, stiff body of a young black man who this world had decided could just be disposable, whose head was shaved and whose legs were burned by electrodes and who was dressed in a suit for the first time in many years and shut in a grey box forever.
>
> We were Ivon Ray Stanley's family. We were Jubilee Community and the Open Door Community; we were people off the street who had come to oppose the execution. We were refugees from Guatemala and Honduras and El Salvador; we were lawyers and organizers who had worked frantically and lovingly and with commitment

---

26. For more information on Jubilee Partners, http://p13643.typo3server.info/56.0.html.

to try to stop the execution. . . . By grace we gathered to bury Ivon Ray Stanley, our brother, who was remembered, as are all the lowly remembered, by name by our God . . . As we shoveled dirt into that grave, tears mingled with sweat and ran down our faces, and through the blur we could see Jesus there shoveling dirt with us. And He said, "Don't be afraid, my little children. For I have overcome this mean ol' world, this condemning world. I have overcome it with love and until the last day I'll live as a refugee with you and among you." (Davis, 1984)

As the call for vengeance by political leaders and many churches has become more insistent, and the poor more maligned, Murphy relies on her faith to sustain her in the face of insurmountable loss.

We started working with homeless people in 1979, when it was estimated that fifteen hundred people were on the streets of Atlanta, most of whom were men. Within ten years, the number had risen to well over fifteen thousand homeless men, women, and children. Now it is a chronic, entrenched system. Similarly, when I started working in prisons in 1977, there were one-fifth of the number of men, women, and children incarcerated in Georgia that there are today.

In the face of this, I cannot speak of success; the word "faithfulness" is much more apropos. How do we keep going when we realize we are in a losing battle? The most important piece is to have a community, so the failures and the deep sorrow and grief are not borne alone. No individual can bear the crushing, hateful power of this system. We must build community on a local level that reaches far and wide to others who do this work.

Everyone who stays with this work has to find a spiritual well to draw on. Many of our colleagues in anti–death penalty work were raised Christians, but now will have nothing to do with organized religion. It is heartbreaking for me, as part of a community of people struggling to be fierce in our discipleship, to know that the Christian faith is encumbering.

Murphy relates a particularly disturbing revelation about her own denomination as she was sitting with a prisoner awaiting execution.

I was pained as I sat there, Presbyterian pastor to these folks—my parishioners—to realize that . . . the decision to aggressively seek a death sentence was made by a D.A. who was a Presbyterian elder. The courtroom prosecutor, who painstakingly explained to the jury why this man was not worthy of life and who convinced them to kill him, was a Presbyterian elder. Finally, the sentence was handed down and the execution date set by a judge who is a Presbyterian elder. (Gathje, 2002: 316)

Nevertheless, Murphy insists on reclaiming the Biblical tradition.

Our deep spiritual well is the discipleship movement of the vagrant Jesus, the dark-skinned Middle Easterner, the executed convict Jesus. That is the well that sustains us, that helps us find the resurrection that is hidden amidst so much crucifixion.

Murphy then related a recent visit from Andrew, who was seventeen years old when she met him and sentenced to death in Baldwin County. At that time (1978) there were sixty-six people on Georgia's death row, and Murphy addressed a Christmas card to each one, and passed them out to members of her congregation, asking them to add a note. Mary, a music teacher, wrote to Andrew.

After many years of visiting on death row, Mary and Andrew became close friends, and then realized they were in love with each other. Andrew was still under a death sentence, but before his fourth trial, they were married in prison. Thanks to some good organizing in the community where the crime was committed, the venue for his fourth trial was changed, and the jury gave him life. Andrew did another ten years with a perfect prison record, which is almost impossible. In 2004, he finally got out, after twenty-seven years.

Andrew and Mary were here for Thanksgiving dinner not long after he was paroled, and you have never seen two happier people. I feel like Andrew is my younger brother, because he was a scared teenager when I met him. He speaks powerfully about the crime he committed and his life's journey to come to terms with it and be accountable. He is a dear, sweet man, filled with love, mercy, and compassion, and wants nothing but to live his life for the good of all people and to help build the Beloved Community.

If this amazing gift of resurrection had only happened once in my life, it would be enough. But it has happened many times. We have had six people stay in our household who have been exonerated and walked off of death row because they did not commit the crimes for which they were convicted.

There are others who have been executed that I am clear were innocent. And there are still others who are on death row today, innocent or guilty, that may or may not escape the gurney. I count among these resurrections not just those who have gotten off, but those who have gone to their deaths unafraid, with hearts full of thanksgiving and compassion—like Roosevelt Green.

Recently when we were together, Murphy spoke of yet another friend she had accompanied on death row for many years. Before his execution, he was asked if he was ready to die. He responded, "Hell no. I don't want to die, I want to live. I am not *ready* to die . . . but I am *prepared*." This was a significant lesson for Murphy's battle with cancer.

In 1995, when the doctors gave me six to eight months to live, I thought, "I don't want to die. I want to see my daughter finish high school and become an adult. But if I have to die, I have had the best teachers, people who faced a much more cruel death." Though facing execution, they did not sacrifice their dignity, did not hand over their capacity for love and forgiveness. This is what lives inside me.

***

In order for peacemakers to transform conflict or heal the wounds of violation, as we pointed out in volume I (chapter 2), they must first "disturb the peace" of an economic and political system in which power is radically disparate and violence is a tool of social control. This is why Jesus of Nazareth was in continual conflict with the authorities of his time, as he took sides with victims of domination and practiced nonviolent direct action at strategic points. And it is why Ephesians calls on Christians to "expose the works of darkness" (Eph 5:11). As disciples of the Jesus who dismantles every wall that divides, Liz McAlister and Murphy Davis embrace solidarity with those targeted by state violence, and nonviolently confront institutionalized death-dealing with the fierce love of Christ. They proclaim "the many-faceted Sophia of God," the good news of restorative justice and peace, to the highest powers (Eph 3:10).

These remarkable women struggle, as we all do, with the temptation to feel overwhelmed at the violence around us, to retreat into our private lives, to indulge in "compassion fatigue." But they understand that, as the writer Audre Lorde reminded us, "Our silence will *not* protect us." Black, lesbian, and feminist, she knew all about marginalization and invisibility. This less well known African American prophet addressed the problem of denial and resignation in a talk given in Chicago, ten years after King's famous "Beyond Vietnam: A Time to Break Silence" speech was delivered at Riverside Church in 1967.[27] Her words powerfully echoed his: "The

---

27. Lorde's text can be found at www.transformationpublications.com/transformation _of_silence.html. For accounts of her life see Lorde (1996) and De Veaux (2004); on

transformation of silence into language and action is an act of self-revelation, and that always seems fraught with danger."

This is particularly true for women, who are socialized to be seen and not heard. To speak out is to become visible, which brings vulnerability—but this, Lorde argued, is the source of our greatest strength. We can "sit in our safe corners mute as bottles, but we will still be no less afraid . . ." she warned. Or "we can learn to work and speak when we are afraid in the same way we have learned to work and speak when we are tired . . ." When she gave this talk, Lorde was, like Murphy Davis, weary from battling cancer, yet determined to keep working and speaking. And like Liz McAlister, Lorde was unwavering in her commitment to Dr. King's call to integrate the personal and the political.

Liz and Murphy are "women clothed with the sun," strong enough to face the Beast, gentle enough to be ambassadors of reconciliation to the neighborhood poor, the homeless, and the prisoner. Like the cosmic woman in Revelation 12, they have "flown with wings of eagles into the wilderness," and there have been nourished in exemplary communities of resistance, solidarity, and renewal (Rev 12:14).[28]

Lorde's struggle with cancer see Lorde (1985). King's "Beyond Vietnam" speech is found in Washington (1986: 231ff.); see our comments in volume I, chapter 2.

28. For more stories of women and faith see Hollyday (1994), who also adopts this trope from Revelation 12 in her reflections on biblical women and social justice.

7

CONFRONTING HISTORIC INJUSTICE

Truth and Reconciliation

Nothing of the past five hundred years was inevitable. Every raised fist
and brandished weapon was a choice. . . . The decision to censor the
native truth was a choice. The decision to manipulate the knowledge
of American history was a choice. . . . With my relations around me, I
go into mourning—but I go angry, alive, listening, learning, remem-
bering. . . . I do not vanish. I do not forget. I will not let you forget.
—Wendy Rose, Hopi/Me-wuk (1992: 6)

History, despite its wrenching pain
Cannot be unlived, but if faced
With courage, need not be lived again.
—Maya Angelou, "On the Pulse of Morning" (1993)

Stories of past violence and justice denied reside in the bones of the children of both victims and perpetrators, whether acknowledged or not. For
most of us in the dominant culture, the truth of historic crimes is slowly
buried under the heavy soil of denial, rationalization, and amnesia. History
as told by the victors is usually a devised narrative, full of half-truths, cari-
catures, and cover-ups. The story of victims, meanwhile, is dismembered
from the official history of the body politic. One of the most demanding,
yet transforming, tasks of restorative justice and peacemaking today is to
revise and *remember* the past, uncovering a fuller, more inclusive truth, and
listening to the voices of those left out.[1] Healing can come only through

---

1. For a theological discussion of this task and its unique North American characteristics, see Myers (1994: 111ff.).

the difficult and painful labor of exhuming—literally and figuratively—
the bones of these violations.

As the last chapter profiled two women we look to as mentors, so here
we offer testimonies of two men who just as surely help us set our moral
and political compass. These elders are giants among us, fierce in their
quest to vindicate the suffering of their community, patient in their work
to overcome collective amnesia and ambivalence. Like the apostle Paul,
Elder Lawrence and Pastor Johnson understand well the three key aspects
of the divine imperative of reconciliation outlined in 2 Cor 5:16ff.:

- all Christians are invited *and* challenged to act as ambassadors of
  reconciliation;
- it is possible for us to "accept the grace of God in vain" (6:1) by not
  taking initiative to heal wounds and restore justice; and
- "the time is now" for the work of reckoning with histories of
  oppression, exclusion, and violation (6:2).[2]

As pioneers of two different expressions of truth and reconciliation work
on this continent, it is not too much to say that these two ministers are
national treasurers of conscience and compassion.

7A. Lawrence Hart of Return to the Earth

The testimony of Elder Lawrence Hart shows how a deeply entrenched
legacy of oppression toward Native Americans can be challenged and
changed—but only by not letting us forget. His pioneering efforts to
repatriate Native American remains are a compelling and creative expression of contemporary restorative justice. As his biographer, Raylene Hinz-
Penner, puts it, Lawrence "represents a unique bridge to the Cheyenne
peace traditions of an earlier time . . . a dynamic and creative force in the
country for mediation, restoration, conciliation and preservation" (2007:
19). We interviewed Elder Lawrence on February 12, 2007.

Elder Lawrence was raised by his paternal grandparents, John P. Hart
and Corn Stalk, until he was six years old. They taught him to speak Cheyenne and instructed him in traditional ways. John Hart was a missionary
of the Native American Church, and Lawrence would often accompany
his grandfather on his trips. Lawrence's father, Homer, was baptized as
a Mennonite at age seventeen. He worked for the church and the tribe
for forty years in Clinton, Oklahoma, where he was a highly respected
preacher, farmer, and leader. "I have connections to three religions," says

---

2. See our exposition of Paul's vision in 2 Corinthians for "ambassadors of reconciliation" in volume I, chapter 1.

Lawrence: "Our own Cheyenne traditional religion, the Native American church of my grandfather, and my father's . . . Mennonite faith" (Ibid.: 118).

Lawrence married Betty Bartel, a Mennonite with German ancestry, in October 1957. He completed studies at Bethel College in Newton, Kansas, and then at Associated Mennonite Biblical Seminary in Elkhart, Indiana. In 1963, Lawrence and Betty accepted a call to pastor at Koinonia Mennonite Church near Clinton, Oklahoma, where they have served for forty-five years. They have worked tirelessly to preserve Cheyenne culture, history, and tradition, establishing the Cheyenne Cultural Center in 1977, which serves as a community center for history, art, language, and interpretation. Betty and Lawrence have three children and four grandchildren.

Lawrence Hart

Photo credit: Cyrus McCrimmon, *Rocky Mountain News*, with permission of Lawrence and Betty Hart photo collection

Over the years Lawrence has garnered a number of honors, including Indian Elder of the Year from the National Indian Education Association; the Oklahoma Heritage Association's Distinguished Service Award; and Friend of the Oklahoma Supreme Court. But it is his work as a peace chief that is most significant to him and to our story.

i. Everything I Do Is from My Stance as a Peace Chief

The Cheyenne have an unbroken line of peace chiefs, since their cultural hero, Sweet Medicine, institutionalized the "Council of Forty-four" many years ago. A chief was chosen from each of the ten Cheyenne bands, along with four additional principal chiefs. Lawrence's grandfather John was one of these peace chiefs.[3]

Despite being raised Mennonite, Lawrence served in the Navy and Marines from 1954 to 1958. "He believed he was the first full-blooded Native American to make it as a jet fighter pilot" (Ibid.: 109). But Sweet Medicine had said that a great peace chief must have a conversion experience, since most were at one time warriors. John Hart was nearing the end of his life, and approached the council with the unusual request

---

3. On the Cheyenne peace chief tradition generally see Hoig (1980); on Black Kettle in particular, see Hatch (2004).

that Lawrence take his place as a principal peace chief, and they agreed. "Being so close emotionally to his grandfather, Lawrence could not say no. He took it as a call. But one cannot be a peace chief and continue to be a warrior. . . . Four months after he was made a principal peace chief of the Cheyenne people, Lawrence was out of the service" (Hinz-Penner, 2002: 117).

Over the past fifty years Lawrence has never experienced a full Council of Forty-four, because as older chiefs pass on it is challenging to find replacements. Few are willing to live by the stringent requirements made by Sweet Medicine, such as this:

> Listen to me carefully and truthfully follow my instructions. You Chiefs are peacemakers. Though your son might be killed in front of your tepee, you should take a peace pipe and smoke. . . . If your men, your soldier societies, should be scared and retreat, you are not to step back but take a stand to protect your land and people. Get out and talk to the people. If strangers come, you are the ones to give presents to them and invitations. . . . Never refuse. (Hoig, 1980: 7)

A peace chief is to be a person of peace no matter what the cost, being available for discernment, encouragement, and intervention. He must recognize what is required for healing his people and land, and use his influence to address those needs, acting as tribal negotiator and spokesperson. It is courageous and demanding work.

Elder Lawrence speaks often of a powerful turning point in his life, in which he was mentored by elder peace chiefs. It occurred at the centenary of the 1868 Washita massacre, the victims of which are his direct ancestors.

> In the 1860s the Cheyenne met the most difficult decade in our history. Even though our peace chiefs had made great efforts to be at peace with the U.S. Government, it proved futile. In 1864, our village at Sand Creek was attacked; many of our people were killed. Four years later, Lieutenant Colonel George Custer and the 7th Cavalry attacked our people again at the Washita. My great-grandfather, Afraid of Beavers, was fairly young and survived the attack. When the Cavalry left, he came out of hiding and, with other survivors, began to look for people. As they walked over the bodies they called out the names of those who had been killed. They found Chief Black Kettle and his wife, Medicine Woman, in the river. They laid their bodies under a cottonwood tree until the next morning, when they took them away and buried them at an undisclosed location. A few

years after the massacre, Afraid of Beavers had a son, John P. Hart, who is my grandfather.[4]

One hundred years later, the white residents of Cheyenne, Oklahoma, near the massacre site, decided to celebrate the "Battle of Washita." They contacted Elder Lawrence, asking for the Cheyenne people to participate. Lawrence responded that they could not celebrate what occurred at Washita.

But the townspeople were persistent. After conversation with other chiefs, Lawrence negotiated that the Cheyenne would participate in the event on one condition. Several years earlier, the remains of one of the victims of the massacre had been unearthed by erosion, and the townspeople had put them on display in a local museum, which was offensive to the Cheyenne. If the chiefs were allowed to take back the remains and reinter them, the Cheyenne would take part in the commemoration.

So it was set. We would set up our tepees and have a mock village filled with our own children and elders. The townspeople would dress up in blue uniforms and undergo a mock attack on our village. After the attack we would proceed downtown and inter the remains. It was difficult to rehearse the event but we planned that as the fake gunshots rang out, we would pretend to be hit and fall down.

On November 29, 1968, the day of the commemoration, I was on the hillside and could see my children in the village. The mock attack began. I saw to my right some young men dressed in blue uniforms with the 7th Cavalry insignia. I had not been told about these young fellows, who called themselves the "Grandsons of the 7th Cavalry," Custer's regiment. They marched towards the village, playing the familiar battle tune of "Gary Owen." With their authentic, carbine weapons, they began to fire blanks into the village. It became so terrifyingly real. I did not want those grandsons to be there, shooting at my children and fellow tribal members. Who invited them? And why were we not told? I began to harbor feelings that I knew I shouldn't have as one of the young peace chiefs. There was screaming, chaos, and gunfire until it was over.

The day's closing ceremony at the Black Kettle Museum, where the chiefs had prepared the historic remains for burial, involved four special

---

4. Elder Lawrence recounted this story at Fresno Pacific University Center for Peacemaking and Conflict Studies' Seventh Annual Restorative Justice Conference, February 25-26, 2000.

songs for their recessional. Much to Lawrence's dismay, as they began singing, the grandsons of Colonel Custer's regiment ceremoniously "presented arms."

> I thought, "How dare they salute this one!" Intense feelings of hatred surfaced. As we walked through a large group of people, a Cheyenne woman stepped forward and removed a beautiful wool blanket from around her shoulders and draped it over the coffin. This act was unplanned, and it required another ritual to acknowledge this gift, which would need to be given to someone else that day. I was thinking the blanket would go to the governor or another state dignitary that was present. Then the chiefs told me to call the captain of the Grandsons of the 7th Cavalry. They handed me the blanket and told me to give it to him. I complied, because I was not going to question my elders. The captain came towards us in sharp military fashion, drew his sword and saluted us. I stepped forward and draped the blanket over his shoulders. It was one of the most powerful moments in my life. There was not a dry eye in the audience.
>
> The chiefs went back into the museum and the Grandsons followed us in—young men in their early twenties, with tears in their eyes. The captain approached me and we embraced, crying. He took a pin from his uniform and said, "Lawrence, this is the 'Gary Owen' pin worn by original members of the 7th Cavalry. It is the signal to attack. I have taken it off my uniform and I want you to have it on behalf of the Cheyenne people. We are sorry that 'Gary Owen' was played that day one hundred years ago, and never again will it be played against your people." I still have that pin. It reminds me less of his words than of the actions of my elders, who showed me that day what it really means to be a peace chief.

"Everything I do," says Elder Lawrence, "is from my stance as a peace chief."

Lawrence was instrumental in establishing Washita as a designated National Historic Site.

> Twice I testified in Congress for the national park at Washita. I believe it is good when the National Park Service manages a site like that because it allows us to tell our side of the story. They are in the process of building an interpretive center. All of the remains associated with the Washita site that have been unearthed by development or by inadvertent discoveries have been reburied right near those grounds.

It is this work of repatriating Indian remains and giving proper burial that lies at the heart of Elder Lawrence's work.

ii. Laying the Past to Rest with Dignity

Chief Lawrence has also been involved in working toward appropriate commemoration and repatriation of remains from the Sand Creek massacre, as the following narrative explains.

Nov. 29, 1864, Sand Creek, Colorado. It was a time of fiercely proud Cheyenne warriors, broken treaties, gold-greedy whites, bloody Indian raids and civil war. On the morning of the attack, it was cold. Everyone in the peaceful Cheyenne camp was asleep in blankets and buffalo robes.

Col. John Chivington and the First Colorado Regiment broke the quiet with rifle fire. Cheyenne chief White Antelope ran to stop the soldiers. He believed the attack was a mistake, because the village had already surrendered to the Army just weeks before and had been promised the army's protection. He cried out in English: "Stop! Stop!" When he saw that it was a deliberate attack, he stood still and began to sing his death song. He was one of the first to be shot down. Desperate to stop the attack, Cheyenne peace chief Black Kettle raised an American flag and a white flag of surrender at his tepee. But the guns wouldn't stop. Soldiers shot down women and children, killed babies in their mother's arms. Scalps were taken; private parts like breasts and testicles were cut off to make tobacco pouches.

Finally the guns fell silent. More than 150 Cheyenne, mostly women and children were dead. Ten Cavalrymen were killed. Army and Congressional inquiries would later call the attack a massacre. Chivington resigned his commission in dishonor. The fields of Sand Creek were heavy with the bodies of the dead . . .

November, 1997, Smithsonian Institute, Washington, D.C. For over 100 years the remains have been in the storage area of the Smithsonian. Back in the 1860s army surgeons had gathered the remains. . . . The rifle was evolving rapidly on the heels of the Civil War, and surgeons were very interested in studying the effects of the new weapons on the human body. For a century the Cheyenne had grieved the wandering souls of Sand Creek, longing to bring them home to give them rest.

An Indian crier begins his song to call the Cheyenne tribe together. He is a long way from Oklahoma. His song echoes through the vast corridors of the Smithsonian Institute, where, on dusty storage shelves, the remains of the ancient Cheyenne have been kept. The Cheyenne have come to bring them home. Chief Lawrence Hart offers a blessing, asking the Creator to be with them as they prepare the dead for the journey home. Visitors are blessed with sage. "God, look down upon us. Grant us your mercy. Our relatives, we are here. We have come for you. We are taking you back home."

There is a horrible silence as the Cheyenne see, for the first time, remains of their ancestors. Then the drum begins. One can see the pain of a hundred years on the skulls: bullet holes, signs of scalping. Elders ceremonially prepare the dead, marking the bones with paint made from the earth of their sacred mountain. Bones gathered so long ago for "scientific research."

For a moment each Cheyenne holds one of the dead in his hands. "There is a lot of pain involved here," says one elder, holding back tears. "What they went through. Some of these here have bullet holes on top of their heads. They were not prepared to defend themselves."

Women gather at the side of an adolescent girl killed that November day. Their emotions are uncontrolled. "Whenever she died or whenever her body was taken, there would have been no one holding her, because of all the chaos and people running for their lives. She never would have had anyone in all these years to hold her like that. She deserved it."

With tears and cedar incense the young girl's remains are placed in a small coffin. It is a swirl of emotions: outrage at the massacre, a sense of violation that the remains had been in a museum for these decades. Everyone is straining towards home, where there is rest for the bitter feelings.[5]

In the 1860s the U.S. surgeon general and the U.S. Army Medical Museum circulated requests for troops on the frontier to collect Native American skulls. It is estimated that between six hundred thousand and two million skeletal remains were subsequently shipped to public and private museums, societal collections, scientific laboratories, and universities across the country for study and storage. "After each massacre or battle medical personnel would collect the remains," Lawrence told us. "Today

---

5. From a slightly edited transcript of "The Long Journey Home," a video produced by Mennonite Central Committee (1997), with footage from segments of Fox 5 News Tonight with reporter Jane Brayden.

decapitating the remains of an enemy and shipping the crania far away for 'scientific study' would be considered a war crime."

Two laws were passed to begin addressing this horrific injustice. The National Museum of the American Indian Act (1989) focused on museums maintained by the Smithsonian Institute, and the Native American Graves Protection and Repatriation Act (NAGPRA, 1990) required museums or universities that have received federal funds to repatriate Native American remains and cultural objects.

> After NAGPRA was passed, the chiefs gathered and I was asked to serve as liaison and work to repatriate our people's remains. I did museum consultation, repatriation, and assisted in burials under both acts. One repatriation in particular stands out in my memory. When the Northern Cheyenne repatriated the remains of ancestors who had died at Fort Robinson, they invited me, a Southern Cheyenne, to come to the Smithsonian Museum of Natural History, where they were stored. During that time, I became acquainted with the Keeper of the Sacred Hat, Joseph Black Wolf. When they were ready to bury the remains at the Two Moon cemetery in Busby, Montana, they invited us to come and take part in the burial ceremony. Mr. Black Wolf was to lead his people as they carried the remains on a one-mile walk to the cemetery grounds. He wanted four people to walk beside him, two on his left and two on his right, and asked if I would be one of those four. The other three were Northern Cheyenne. It was an honor I will never forget, and further inspired me to continue my work of repatriation.

In 1995, Lawrence was appointed by then interior secretary Bruce Babbitt to serve on the review committee of NAGPRA, which included monitoring implementation, resolving disputes, and making annual reports to Congress. He helped tribal groups that could not agree on who should steward remains to resolve their differences in traditional ways, rather than through litigation.

Many remains are now being repatriated by tribes who can lay claim to them. But because of disregard for how remains were collected and stored, and because of poor record keeping, many remains cannot be identified. Scientists are able to determine gender and approximate age, but cannot establish tribal identity. The NAGPRA office at the Department of Interior has been accepting inventories of stored remains from museums and universities around the United States, and their database now lists over 118,000 culturally unidentifiable remains. During the eight years Lawrence served on the review committee, he worked on recommendations for the disposition of these remains, which are now being made into rules and regulations.

> One of the recommendations we made was to establish dedicated burial grounds to receive culturally unidentified remains only. These cemeteries will always be a reminder of this part of our history as a nation. The federally recognized tribes should take the lead in determining where these cemeteries will be located. Some wanted to use federal lands controlled by the Bureau of Land Management or the U.S. Forest Service. But others felt that tribes need to be responsible to find a place to bury the remains, and not depend on the U.S. government. I agreed with the latter rationale, recommending that tribes try to establish regional cemeteries throughout the U.S.

The National Congress of American Indians, the largest and oldest Native organization in the United States, is helping organize regional coalitions to establish such cemeteries.

Lawrence committed to help establish the first cemetery in Clinton, Oklahoma, which could serve as a model for other regional sites. On April 3, 2007, at his invitation, thirty-nine federally recognized tribal leaders and designated NAGPRA personnel came to Clinton to dedicate a new building at the Cheyenne Cultural Center, and to walk the proposed grounds for the cemetery. There the Southern Tier High Plains Coalition was formed to be responsible for all the unidentifiable remains and objects in their area, and it will contact museums and universities in Colorado, Kansas, Missouri, Arkansas, Texas, Louisiana, and Oklahoma, which hold an estimated twenty-three thousand unidentifiable remains. The cemetery in Clinton will be large enough to hold all of these remains.

The process has been slow, as tribes concentrate on repatriating culturally identifiable objects and remains. In 2005, Lawrence founded the Return to the Earth project (RTE), whose mission is to

> support Native Americans in burying unidentifiable ancestral remains now scattered across the United States and enable a process of education and reconciliation between Native and Non-Native peoples. RTE envisions an ecumenical effort developing regional burial sites throughout Indian country supported by people of faith and governed by diverse, regional Native committees.[6]

---

6. For more information see: www.rfpusa.org/returntotheearth/index.html.

The horror of the massacres and the human dismemberment that followed is, Lawrence states, "a gross injustice that needs to be corrected." He is enlisting the help of faith-oriented groups who believe in peace and justice (RTE is fiscally sponsored by Mennonite Central Committee U.S.). In the process of contacting MCC constituents, a couple of church groups offered land for other possible burial grounds, which Hart calls "a gracious and wonderful gift."

> I am glad that faith-based people who believe in restorative justice are coming forward to be a part of Return to the Earth. This whole project operates under the mantra of restorative justice. I approached MCC first because of the Mennonites' strong stance on peace and justice. The U.S. Conference of Religions for Peace (www.rfpusa .org) includes about seventy different groups, and they have indicated they will participate as well. RTE is a massive, multi-year project that will be expensive, and we are avoiding federal funding. So we are depending on the goodwill of all faith-based groups.

Elder Lawrence hopes RTE will become important to churches, which in turn will organize local study programs, facilitate fund-raising efforts, and distribute RTE materials.

A centerpiece of the project is the invitation to congregations to build cedar boxes and sew muslin cloths to be used to transport and bury remains.

> As congregants are building boxes they also write litanies and prayers. We ask them to hold a special dedication for these boxes, and to be mindful as they are sent off to the MCC warehouse. The congregation helps cover transportation costs. Not long ago, after I described the cedar boxes to an audience, an art student came up and asked if she could make a hard-fired clay box of the same dimensions. I answered positively. Now several students from her class are going to make similar special boxes. Perhaps remains of children or adolescents will be buried in these boxes.
>
> We are asking non-Native congregations throughout the U.S. who build these boxes to also invite descendents of the Native Americans who were displaced from that particular place to participate. Two churches in Beatrice, Nebraska, have researched the tribes that historically occupied that region and invited descendents to become acquainted. My hope is that through this project, reconciliations between Native and non-Native peoples will begin taking place all over the U.S.

Hart has experienced some resistance from fellow Native Christians concerning the use of traditional rituals and ceremonies in the preparation and burial of remains.

> Some have admonished me saying, "If you are going to leave Jesus Christ out of this, you are not going to get our support." I have tried to reason with them, explaining that it is fine that they bury their people today with Christian ritual. But the people who were killed in the 1860s had never heard the Good News of Jesus Christ. It is better that we allow the traditional people to use their ceremonies. When we buried the remains of our ancestors killed at Sand Creek, we had to remember that they were killed by *Christians*. We used our traditional ways and that is appropriate. It is disappointing to me that some of our own Native brothers and sisters will not support this project because of that, but I am okay with it.

In the past decade the restorative justice movement has begun to acknowledge and rediscover the many traditions of wisdom that indigenous people were using prior to contact.

> *The Cheyenne Way* (Llewellyn, Ross, and Hoebel, 2002) is used in conflict-resolution classes and some law schools across our nation. It clearly shows that the Cheyenne peace chiefs practiced restorative justice. We have many stories in our oral tradition about how we dealt with offenders. For example, during the 1860s, a three-hundred-member tribal group under the leadership of Chief Dull Knife and Chief Little Wolf were fleeing from the U.S. military. They came over a small hill and at the bottom saw white buffalo hunters skinning the animals. The Cheyenne despised the buffalo hunters because they slaughtered the buffalo and took only the hides, leaving the rest of the carcass to rot. The tribal members surrounded the buffalo hunters, who thought their fate was sealed. But the peace chiefs sat down, took out a pipe, and smoked, talking between themselves. When they had finished the ritual, they told their young men to let the buffalo hunters go. It was the chief's way of saying, "We are peacemakers, and no matter the cost we will not harm these buffalo hunters."

I marvel at how our people came to use restorative justice. People who were at one time banished from the tribe were always restored after months or perhaps a few years—much like the prodigal son was restored in the Gospel. So I believe that recovering and giving proper burial to our ancestral remains is a good example of what a contemporary peace chief should do.

7B. Nelson Johnson of the Greensboro Truth and Community Reconciliation Project

Nelson Johnson, preaching in
Philadelphia, 2003.
Photo credit: Word & World,
used with permission

The spirit and power of prophetic African American Christian faith has animated movements for social change many times throughout U.S. history. The most well known expression of this tradition was Dr. Martin Luther King's leadership in the civil rights movement of the 1950s and 60s. We believe that Rev. Nelson Johnson of Greensboro, North Carolina, embodies the character and vision of Dr. King in our generation.

Nelson is deeply grounded in the black freedom movement, and has for five decades been involved in struggles for justice, particularly around issues of race and labor. He is pastor of Faith Community Church, located just across the railroad tracks from downtown Greensboro. His church houses a number of grassroots initiatives in this low-income, African American neighborhood. A powerful preacher and teacher, Nelson interprets the story of Jesus and its relevance to the present struggle for cultural and economic equality each week with his small congregation. Nelson speaks with the moral authority of someone who has been profoundly victimized by racism: stabbed by would-be assassins, jailed on trumped up charges, targeted by the police, and maligned by the political establishment. Yet his countenance bears none of this; indeed, as a community organizer he is more interested in helping residents find *their* voice and tell their stories. Most importantly for our focus, Nelson has animated the historic Greensboro Truth and Community Reconciliation Project, the first such effort to take place on U.S. soil.

Nelson has been married to Joyce Johnson since 1969, a woman of equal courage and commitment. Joyce was among the first African American students to graduate from Duke University in 1968, and has worked for black liberation in the United States and Africa and for quality public education, economic justice, and women's rights. She retired in 2000 after twenty-seven years of service to North Carolina Agricultural and Technical State University, where she was director of the Transportation Institute. Joyce now directs the Jubilee Institute, which is part of the Beloved Community Center, the hub of Nelson's work in Greensboro.[7] We interviewed Nelson in January, 2006.

i. Decoding a "Culture of Civility": From the Sit-Ins to the Klan Massacre

Nelson grew up in Littleton, North Carolina, a small Southern town of eight hundred people and hometown of the great civil rights activist Ella Baker. He listened to his mother tell stories of "the white man," some of which were in the realm of mythology, but some of which were strict accounts of what happened to somebody.

> There was a farm on Route 4 out of Littleton where large numbers of black folks worked. It had acres and acres of land and was owned by a white farmer, Bernice West. Black people worked on that land all week, they were pushed hard. On Saturdays they would come into town for a day of relief and release. There was a little juke joint with heavy beat music, and sometimes people got a little too juiced. That's when experiences with the police would occur.
>
> As a child I would go to town on Saturday afternoons and often see a policeman open-hand slap a black man across the face. The police would just pull the man's collar and slap him for some offense, like public drunkenness, and then haul him off to jail. But no matter what Bernice West's workers did, West would come, take some of the black man's money, pay a little to the court, grease a few palms, and get him out of jail, so he could be back to work on his farm on Monday. Anyone who wasn't a part of West's farm would stay in jail and get the book thrown at them. It was a good-old-boy network, and it deeply enforced the pattern of behavior among all parties.
>
> When a black person went to court, they knew their word would not be taken against that of a white person. The death of a black person only got reasonable adjudication if it were another black person who killed them. If a white person murdered a black person, justice did not follow. Black farmers who owned their land and tried to get a loan to put in crops got the higher interest rate. These kinds of things

7. For more information see: www.belovedcommunitycenter.org.

were rooted in a way of life, and they only got addressed when they passed a certain point of tolerance. In other words, there was a level of normality to this racial oppression. It was all within a "culture of acceptability."

These experiences anchored Nelson in an understanding of the domination system.

As a young person he couldn't figure out why people didn't get together and resist this system. His father was president of the NAACP in a little town called Enfield, and often over meals his parents would talk about the struggle. They were not talking to Nelson, but he was listening. People were doing what they could in those days as the civil rights movement gained energy in the 1950s. But Nelson remembers thinking consciously, "I'm going to do something about this system when I grow up."

Raised in the Baptist Church, as a child Nelson embraced the ideals of his family and the church. During the 1960s, he was deeply impacted by the work of Dr. Martin Luther King, Jr.

> I had Dr. King's records, and listened to them hundreds of times, feeling the depth of his spirit. I had a friend who ran a sound company in Greensboro, and we would rent a big speaker, put it on top of our truck and play Martin's recordings throughout the community. Even after I came to disagree with what I thought was Martin's flawed logic of nonviolence, I never dismissed him or questioned his integrity.

Nelson was in high school when the famous inaugural sit-in took place at the Greensboro Woolworth's on February 1, 1960.[8] There was a palpable fervor and energy among African American youth, and Nelson felt it.

At age sixteen, with great fear and trembling, Nelson and a friend went to Trevi Fountain Restaurant on Main Street in Littleton. It had wicker chairs and tables, and Nelson and his friends had longed to order a soda and sit in those chairs, like white folks did.

> We were so nervous; it's hard for me to capture the dimension of fear that exists when you move past a certain point in the "normative culture." For us that point was buying a soda and sitting in those wicker chairs at Trevi Fountain. The owner came over, looked at us, and said, "You boys know better than this. Get up and get the hell out of here!" And we did. It was deeply painful to experience that

---

8. For history and background on the sit-in movement, the best sources are Chafe (1981) and Hogan (2007). See also www.sitins.com

and feel no recourse or capacity to do anything about it because it was all legal and acceptable.

Having seen and experienced this kind of discrimination repeatedly, Nelson became part of the movement of the early 1960s that resisted the culture of Jim Crow, articulating the injustice of that system and engaging its practices, customs, and laws.

In the late 1960s, Nelson attended North Carolina Agricultural and Technical State University, a black college in Greensboro. In March 1969, he successfully organized NCA&T students to support striking cafeteria workers in their struggle to win better pay and working conditions. Shortly after, Nelson was elected student government vice president. In May, NCA&T student leaders became involved in a struggle at nearby Dudley High School.[9]

> Dudley was in the middle of student elections, and the majority of students wanted to elect Claude Barnes as student body president, but his name was not allowed on the ballot. But the students wrote in Claude's name on the ballots, and he won an overwhelming victory. Yet the all-white Board of Education refused to allow Claude to be seated because, they said, he was part of a subversive black organization. Barnes, you see, was raising issues of educational equity and racial justice in his platform.

When Barnes and eight friends began picketing out in front of the school, the police came and beat and arrested them. This occurred during class break, and hundreds of Dudley students saw the violence. A large group went over to the NCA&T campus, where Nelson and others were holding a national Student Organization for Black Unity conference. The college students immediately dropped what they were doing and went to join their younger brothers and sisters, marching back to Dudley with hundreds of others joining them on the way. There they were joined by other black activists, including some Vietnam veterans. The demonstration eventually moved back over to the NCA&T campus, where the National Guard, brought in to quell a "riot," stormed the campus with tanks, tear gas, and gunfire, penning the demonstrators into the dorms. One student was killed, and many, including five police officers, were injured.

---

9. For background to this and other incidents mentioned in Nelson's testimony, see the accounts of Bermanzohn (2003) and Waller (2002), who are fellow survivors of the 1979 Greensboro Massacre. For a compelling personal narrative of parallel events during this period in nearby Oxford, North Carolina—just a few miles from where Nelson grew up—see Tyson (2004).

Nelson called a meeting with all of the black ministers in town to plead with the Dudley High School principal, who was himself black, to meet and resolve the situation. But the principal refused to come because the Board of Education forbade him.

The high school principal became a colonial representative in the school as someone who was subject to the will of the dominant culture rather than to his own community. The whole Greensboro community reacted in the wake of this uprising, which polarized the city. While the powers demonized me, I was exalted by others in the black community. The public discussion labeled us "Black Panthers"—it was all framed in terms of race, even as people were denying it was a racial incident. A report, written later by the Civil Rights Commission under the leadership of the legendary lawyer Julius Chambers, was scathingly critical of how the city reacted. But Greensboro had this deeply developed "Southern sensibility of civility," where people don't talk plainly but just tip their hats and dip and bow—until dark comes, that is. That's when people get hung.[10]

During these years, Nelson became disillusioned with the church because of the way that so many people did not "live up to Christian standards." He began experimenting with different philosophical groundings.

I went through a period where I tried some other things, Marxism in particular. But after a while that well ran dry, not in its logic, but in its ability to fuel my soul. Marxist beliefs animated good work, and the movements were never without spirit. Whenever we got together in the Communist Workers Party we would sing songs, for example, and people really cared for each other. But there wasn't a theology, or the work of a person who embodied it all.

Meanwhile, the civil rights movement had broken down certain discriminatory employment laws, and by the 1970s it was possible for black people to be hired in local mills.

Nelson became deeply involved in textile factory organizing, as well as continuing with community work. It was a familiar reality in the mills:

---

10. This "culture of civility" has been explored by Chafe (1981), who traces the history of Greensboro from 1940 to 1970 and its role in launching several national movements. He shows how the white power structure, while attempting to maintain a progressive mystique, systematically avoided, undercut, or attempted to divide the Greensboro freedom struggle—which continues to the present day.

black workers were the last hired, first fired, and worst treated.[11] But in fact, no one in the mills was doing well; white workers had their problems and complaints too. It was the potential for white and black workers to talk and organize together that Nelson hoped to mobilize.

> Power is always involved in intersecting layers of oppression, such as race, gender, and class. I talk a lot about race because it is the dominant experience in my life as an African American. We see through the glasses we wear, and that have been imposed on us to wear. But in Greensboro we have constantly had to reckon with the concurrent and overlapping power dimension of economic class.
>
> In 1974, I went to my first union meeting at Proximity Print Works, a textile plant that printed beautiful cloths. There were about seven people at the meeting, all older white males. They were not talking about anything that seemed transformative to me, and there weren't any black people there. Soon afterwards, I developed and circulated a leaflet that compared the salary of the highest paid CEO and the lowest-paid worker. It read, "Do you think that what the CEO does is worth so much more than what you do?" This was pretty easy arithmetic, and it invited people into lively discussion. Of course, this brought resentment from management, because we were challenging the particular issues of wage justice *and* the whole culture among the mills.
>
> At the same time, the issue of race was also woven into this reality. In some ways the community was beginning to overcome the Jim Crow mentality, but race was being used as a divisive tactic in the mill. Gender issues were also articulated in terms of who got what jobs and how much men and women were paid.

By 1979, they had become relatively successful in organizing textile mills, drawing about ninety people, black and white, to union meetings. They were building a strong, unified base to challenge mill leadership, and hoped to further address unjust labor practices and racism.

On November 3, 1979, Nelson and other labor organizers from the Workers' Viewpoint Organization (later renamed the Communist Workers Party) were preparing for a legal rally through a working-class black neighborhood in Greensboro. People slowly gathered to begin the demonstration; children and senior citizens were coming out of the housing

---

11. For a comprehensive narrative of the relationship between African American struggles for labor and racial justice throughout this period, see Honey (1999).

projects to join in the singing and preparations for the march. Suddenly, a caravan of nine cars carrying Ku Klux Klan and American Nazi Party members drove toward the organizers. The Klansmen stopped, calmly pulled weapons out of the trunks of their cars and opened fire. In eighty-eight seconds, they killed five labor and community organizers: César Cauce, Dr. Mike Nathan, Bill Sampson, Sandi Smith, and Dr. Jim Waller. Ten others were wounded, including Nelson. The attackers escaped serious injury and most fled the scene unhindered.

Nelson had obtained a parade permit from the city, but only on the condition that he sign a document stating that none of the demonstrators would carry weapons. He had been assured of police escorts. But all of the police assigned to the parade were sent to lunch early, just before the Klan and Nazis arrived. It was learned later that the Greensboro Police Department was fully aware of the Klan's plans, and their own paid informant, Klansman Eddie Dawson, was a leader in the confrontation.

Despite the fact that four television crews had captured the killings on film, the perpetrators were acquitted by all-white juries in two separate trials. Eventually, a 1985 federal civil suit brought by survivors of the shooting found—for the first time in U.S. history—Klan and Nazi members as well as Greensboro police jointly liable for one of the deaths. The City paid a $351,000 settlement, but has never apologized or acknowledged any wrongdoing.[12]

The aftermath of the events shows how the power of domination works through deception and "spin." The day after the massacre, local newspapers reported that Klansmen had attacked a legally scheduled parade. Within two days, the papers had changed their position, stating that the incident was a "shoot-out" between two extremist groups from outside of Greensboro. The labor organizers were demonized as Communists, and Nelson labeled as the "most dangerous man in Greensboro." Jim Melvin, Greensboro's mayor in 1979, asserted that the city had no race-relation problems "except for the ones Nelson Johnson manufactured." Many organizers lost their jobs and were unable to find work for years. The entire city has suffered from the impact of this tragedy; and because there is no common understanding about the events, they continue to serve as a basis for fear, division, and distrust.

---

12. The settlement became the seed money for the Greensboro Justice Fund, which has since pursued a mission of keeping the story of the massacre alive as well as resourcing grassroots social justice organizing in the region; see www.gjf.org. For personal accounts of survivors see Bermanzohn (2003) and Waller (2002),

ii. From Death to Resurrection: Toward Beloved Community

In the wake of the post-massacre trials, Nelson was isolated, maligned, and thoroughly demonized by those who were still fearful of his organizing, and was avoided by people in his own community who were afraid to associate with him. Only two preachers visited him during his time in jail—one black and one white. Their conversations stimulated a new look at his childhood faith.

> This isolation forced me to reflect on what I should do. I went to Mississippi for five months to work with Jesse Jackson's presidential campaign in 1984. But there was something in me that wanted to stay in Greensboro to wrestle this thing out. I started going to church, wandering from congregation to congregation. The first thing that struck me was how warmly I was received in the black churches. People hugged me and asked me how I was doing. Aside from the little network of people within the Communist Workers Party, I wasn't getting a lot of affirmation, and then only very privately. The public acceptance in the churches made me feel good, and it got me reflecting on Jesus.
>
> There was an older black pastor who was deeply spiritual but plain spoken—he'd never be accused of being a powerful preacher in the African American tradition! But his account of the prodigal son impacted me powerfully. I identified with it and began reading the gospels. I saw dimensions of Jesus I hadn't noticed before: how he confronted people and challenged systems of oppression. Because church talk about crucifixion is overly theologized, I had never realized that the cross was the consequence of Jesus' political resistance.
>
> I wanted to know what sustained Jesus in his ministry, and how his sense of reality transcended the status quo. He had a certain unshakeable confidence that while the things of our world may come and go, there is a greater force at work, and even death cannot bring it to an end. I was comforted by that and felt called into this way of being.

Nelson moved to Richmond and lived with his in-laws so he could attend Virginia Union School of Theology. On weekends, Nelson traveled back to Greensboro to be with Joyce and their two daughters, who were completing high school. Although challenging for the family, school offered a welcome break.

> Seminary was a very enjoyable three years. I wasn't being called at all hours of the night, I wasn't in court, or having to duck the police.

Unlike some students, I focused fairly narrowly on Jesus in my studies (I now recognize that I need to work more on the Hebrew Bible). I was in the library reading stories that I didn't know existed, and in vigorous discussions and even arguments with students and professors in class. They all knew about the 1979 Massacre, and asked, "What in the world were you doing that for?" And I had to wrestle with them and explain my motivations.

It was during that period that Nelson went to visit a Klan member in a spirit of reconciliation. "It was one of several times," Joyce told us, "that I kissed Nelson goodbye and wondered if I would ever see him again."

After seminary, Nelson returned home and began again organizing around labor and community issues, now with new convictions about discipleship, nonviolence, and the role of the church. Increasingly he looked to Dr. Martin Luther King as a source of inspiration and direction. In 1991, Nelson and African American community members with whom he was working, together with two white Presbyterian ministers, Barbara Dua and Zee Holler, founded the Beloved Community Center. The BCC has become a remarkable hub for community and regional organizing that is committed to "affirming and realizing the equality, dignity, worth, and potential of every person, and to confronting the systems of domination that prevent us from doing so."[13]

In 1996, I led a group of ministers to become involved with K-Mart workers in Greensboro in their struggle for a living wage. In that campaign, my own growth in, and articulation of, nonviolence matured. We were able to bring together deeply adversarial forces within and outside of the union movement, encouraging them to see each other not as the enemy, but as a beloved community. We persuaded union organizers that they needed to give priority to building allies in the community, and church leaders to recognize that their congregants were workers too. While it wasn't a perfect collaboration, ultimately the workers won the best first contract in the history of North Carolina.

During this period Nelson also began pastoring Faith Community Church, located in a building shared with the BCC. Members of this small congregation work with homeless folks in the neighborhood, and have recently begun a community garden.

Nelson has developed a keen analysis of how power and privilege is pat-

---

13. For more information on this extraordinary network and its kaleidoscope of creative projects, see www.belovedcommunitycenter.org.

terned locally, regionally, and nationally, and its relationship to historical spirals of violence (above, chapter 1).

> Reality is made up of a web of particularities, but when the culture demands that we only acknowledge isolated incidents, our ability to grasp the pattern of a system is diminished. One of the things I discovered early on is that the modus operandi of the powers is never to concede a general pattern of injustice. When people try to name the pattern, the powers claim it was just an isolated event. Their mantra is, "This incident has nothing to do with race and nothing to do with justice. This is just one small and anomalous occurrence." The powers are then able to scapegoat the parties involved, and sometimes that can even be a white person. The whole culture participates and endorses the injustice, but individuals are blamed.
>
> If someone pushes to address the pattern of abuse, the culture and the powers demonize that person. I used to think of this phenomenon as irrational and evil, and it may be, but I'm not sure that is the best way to think about it. Now I believe that the dominant culture is itself profoundly traumatized, and when we push against it we are inviting the culture to look into its own history of trauma. For European Americans this means looking all the way back to their ancestors—many of whom were prisoners or bond-servants—who came to the New World to escape the abuses in their own countries. Because they didn't face their own displacement and abuse, they could only inflict it on others, thus embedding trauma in the new culture they were building, even as they were proclaiming their liberation from it.
>
> How else can we explain slavery? How else do we shed light on a people who understand themselves as the cradle of democracy while denying democracy to whole communities, and who then unleash a mountain of brutality to enforce and maintain their privilege? I am increasingly persuaded that our country represents an experience in traumatic mutuality: the traumatized are a mirror for the culture of domination, which is itself traumatized. I am beginning to understand that this is what we are involved in here.

With this in mind, Nelson recognized that Greensboro could never move forward with racial or economic justice if it did not face the truth of the November 3 Massacre. So, despite his full plate of church and organizing commitments, he helped spearhead a community coalition that launched the Greensboro Truth and Community Reconciliation Project (GTCRP), which began in 2001.

In retrospect, I question whether we were wise in our explicit challenges to the Klan; we advertised our 1979 protest as a "Death to the Klan" rally, and strongly challenged the Klan's efforts to impede our organizing in the mills. I acknowledge that we made significant errors in both our attitude and some of our actions. Yet the fact is, we did not plan to shoot anyone during that march on November 3rd, nor did we shoot anyone. We did not do any of the violent things that were alleged by the authorities. Yet the perception persists. So the question arises: What does one do to help a community work through this level of confusion? That is what led to our exploration of the possibility of a Greensboro Truth and Community Reconciliation Project.[14]

Initially we had a long struggle over whether the project title should include the word "community." One of my concerns was that the role of institutions, like the media, courts, and education system, must be addressed in this process, because these institutions are more basic to the community than the role of any individual. If we only address interpersonal relationships, we might become convinced that we have accomplished transformation, when in fact the social structures remain unchanged.

For example, as a result of the GTCRP, one Nazi member met privately with some of the surviving victims. He felt he was close to death and was seeking a private meeting to clear his conscience. In another instance, I received a phone call from a son of one of the Klan shooters who felt helpless, and I offered him pastoral care. But even if honest healing should transpire between a Klan member and myself, our reconciliation wouldn't necessarily change the community. We might become agents of change, but ultimately the pressing issues of racial and economic justice cannot be eclipsed by personalities. Personalizing the issue is one of the flawed assumptions that have complicated this legacy from the beginning.

The project's first task was an organizing one:

The idea was actively opposed by governmental structures, and by a significant sector of the white population. We had no state subpoena power, and were publicly ridiculed by the white press for daring to raise the 1979 Massacre. Our critics framed the GTCRP as a ploy

---

14. For information and documents concerning the Greensboro Truth and Community Reconciliation Project see www.gtcrp.org. Accounts and analysis can also be found in Cose (2004: 119ff.); Grandin and Klubock (2007: 104ff.); and Martin and Yaquinto (2007).

by survivors to reinject ourselves into the "peace and harmony" of the Greensboro community. In order to move forward we had to build significant consensus around the city.

It was very helpful when Carolyn Allen, who had been city mayor for nine years, threw herself into the process, despite experiencing abuses and demonization. We also had to procure support from the outside, and collaboration with the International Center for Transitional Justice was key. We also received encouragement and participation from several significant actors in the South Africa TRC process: Anglican archbishop Desmond Tutu, Methodist bishop Peter Storey, and Reverend Bongani Finca.[15]

Despite local opposition, the GTCRP was publicly announced during the Martin Luther King holiday in 2002 with a declaration and a mandate explaining why a TRC was necessary. A broad community consultation process followed. In March 2003, the GTCRP invited seventeen different groups, from city officials to grassroots organizations, to name a representative to a committee that would, in turn, select seven commissioners.[16] The commission was sworn in and empanelled on June 12, 2004, by U.S. representative Mel Watt (D-North Carolina), former Greensboro mayor Carolyn Allen, and District Court Judge Lawrence McSwain, with over five hundred people attending to give support and encouragement. Over the next two years, three public hearings were held, and though there was no court order to appear, more than two hundred people presented testimony. This included the judge that presided over the original criminal case, the lawyer for the Klan and the Nazis, the lawyers who won the 1985 civil suit, Klan and Nazi members, survivors, and residents of the traumatized Morningside community. Hundreds of people gathered at these hearings to listen to riveting testimony.

The seven commissioners had to deal with death threats, evidence that

---

15. The ICTJ has facilitated Truth and Reconciliation Commissions all over the world and played an important role in helping the GTCRP conceive and organize its work; see www.ictj.org. Each of the three South African clerics visited and consulted with the GTCRP on numerous occasions. We also had the privilege of serving on the advisory board of the project in its planning stage.

16. Out of those groups, fourteen nominated a representative. The Sons of Confederate Veterans and the United Daughters of the Confederacy immediately declined. The police department and the Chamber of Commerce, after much deliberation, chose not to appoint someone. Any citizen of Greensboro could nominate any person to be a potential commissioner, and sixty-seven people were nominated before the selection committee was formed. Commissioners had to be people of integrity and principle, willing to commit themselves to seek the truth amid all of the data and perspectives, and could not have been directly involved in the events of November 3, 1979.

had been tampered with, FBI reports that had been changed, and filing cabinets that were mysteriously broken into. Still, they persisted with investigative work and community engagement, researching and assessing evidence, records, written literature, and personal statements. On May 25, 2006, they released a 529-page report summarizing their findings, conclusions, and recommendations.[17] This then launched a formal year of discussion of the findings in the City of Greensboro.

> We think the GTCRP, despite those who opposed it or wanted it quickly completed and "behind us," represents the most democratic process in the city's history. Of course, the most difficult part of the journey is ahead of us—though, truth be told, *each* part of this process has seemed more difficult than the one before! Will the Greensboro community be able to hold a serious discussion and acknowledge that the massacre and its aftermath are a result of hundreds of years of race and class degradation, abuse and manipulation? If so, how do we begin a process of healing and restoration? This is where the rubber meets the road, and where something new and beautiful can emerge, even if in a stunted form. These are good seeds being sown.
>
> Will our schools embrace a curriculum that is more rooted in truth and compassion? If the massacre was in fact a result of a system of exploitation, in which some enjoy vast wealth while others strain to make ends meet, how do we reconfigure our collective life in such a way that the possibility of enough for all can emerge? No one can do this for us—the community has to do it for itself, out of a conviction that there is a more excellent way, so we are not forever confined to destructive extremities of wealth and poverty.
>
> The commission report must not end up as some moral treatise with no practical effect. I hope that we will wrestle with these matters in a way that impacts our newspaper, our courts, and all of our children in prison. I hope that this challenging process will animate people whose hearts yearn for personal and political change. I believe that there is something inside of people that longs for a measure of truth, for a way of understanding the Other that holds out hope and possibility.

Archbishop Desmond Tutu, who came to Greensboro on several occasions to support the work of the GTCRP, expressed in a recent meeting with Nelson and Joyce his appreciation for the GTCRP, but also his fears. "Unless Truth and Reconciliation Commissions occur on a mass scale in

---

17. The Executive Summary is available at http://www.gtcrp.org.

the U.S.," he confided, "this wonderful nation is on the road to destruction given its international conduct and behavior."[18] Nelson, too, is hopeful for this work but well aware of the difficulties, and believes that TRCs will not spread in this country unless they are linked to the felt needs of people.

> A public discussion about a historic event that focuses only on culpability—who was right, who was wrong, or whether the government was involved—isn't enough. These are important moral questions, and I am fighting to answer them, but at the end of the day the TRC must lead to a *therefore*: If this be true, what shall we do? People will not rush to embrace something that doesn't make any difference for their lives. That would be like having a good discussion in church about the Bible, but when the flood comes everybody drowns anyway. If behavior doesn't change, if people are still starving, if their children are still going to jail, TRCs will not be embraced. In order for TRCs to avoid becoming domesticated, as have so many other great political innovations, they must stay connected to real life.
>
> We are working to build initiatives around the GTCRP so it will not be splintered by the culture of domination. For example, we are currently gathering twenty thousand signatures in support of a living wage for the local public and private sector. We see this as congruent with the GTCRP, part of the "therefore," the feet walking right beside the truth process.
>
> Another example is our work developing a "plan from below" for our city. There is, of course, a plan from above, called Action Greensboro, and it has mapped out the future of the city—what industry is coming, what gentrification will happen and where. But no such thing exists from the perspective of the poor, who are trapped in the basement of this dysfunctional house. We would hope that the GTCRP will put questions of economic justice on the table, so that the city planning process will face them. The reality of people being excluded from the current global economy has to be examined. Increasingly most of the available jobs are in the service sector, but these jobs don't pay a living wage. A "truth" that doesn't take these issues into account in the public conversation isn't really worth much. Greensboro needs both truth *and* a fair economy.

Nelson has become increasingly interested in facilitating cooperation between labor organizers and clergy, developing an approach he calls

---

18. For his reflections on the South African TRC process and thoughts on related issues, see Tutu (1999).

"community unionism," which has animated his current Southern Faith, Labor and Community Alliance.

> Recently I helped mediate between some of the largest unions in the nation who were in conflict over jurisdiction in North Carolina. Trade-union leadership does not want to fight the clergy because they recognize they do not have the capacity to win anything by themselves—unlike forty years ago, when labor represented 35-40 percent of the work force and had more political clout. As clergy, we recognize we can no longer allow labor organizers to come in and tear up our community over jurisdictional fights. So we met at the Beloved Community Center and reached an agreement: each union signed a document stating that before their organizers move into a city on a campaign, they would submit their plans to a group of clergy for discernment and collaboration. When I shared this result with friends at Interfaith Worker Justice in Chicago, they were pleasantly astounded. We are in an historic moment where labor wants to cooperate with the community, and we have a set of circumstances that make this more possible.[19]

I have a sense that a weakness in the civil rights movement was the fact that Dr. King's disciples were never fully developed because of the overwhelming weight on King as a charismatic leader, as well as the pressure exerted on him by FBI chief J. Edgar Hoover's relentless hounding. Martin was planning to meet with the great Trappist monk Thomas Merton in order to plan a lengthy sabbatical for King to think through how to accomplish training and discipleship. I don't know how King would have accomplished this, since at the time he was deeply involved in the Poor People's Campaign, as well as the sanitation workers' strike in Memphis that ultimately took him to the Cross. But one of my mentors, Dr. Vincent Harding, believes King would have realized that training priority.[20]

---

19. Nelson's vision of community unionism was further developed at two collaborative conferences between the Word and World School and Southern Faith, Labor and Community Alliance: in Memphis (2006) and Tar Heel, NC (2007). Leaders from throughout the South and beyond discussed the problems and possibilities of strategic and Spirit-led collaboration in the work of labor and economics justice. Central to these gatherings was the story of King's solidarity with the Memphis sanitation workers in 1968; see www.wordandworld.org/FaithLaborCommunityAlliance.shtml. We had the pleasure of serving with Nelson on the board of Word and World, an occasional school for faith-based justice and peace activists (see Myers, 2002).

20. See Harding (2008 and 1990). Dr. Harding, spiritual advisor to Dr. King and the foremost historian and interpreter of the civil rights movement and its enduring implica-

I believe that what Martin left undone is now ours to do. We need to gather the descendents of slaves who are called to the gospel and rooted in a tradition that can be reclaimed, in order to energize a broader movement. It doesn't necessarily have to become a mammoth movement, but it does have to be rooted in an unshakeable faith. When something is thus grounded, it is not easily destroyed, and has an influence far beyond its numbers. We have seen this in our work in Greensboro; we don't have overwhelming crowds involved, but we are rooted locally, try to do our work with integrity, and it is having an impact.

My faith thus continues to be a growing dimension of my work. I am persuaded that we can't calculate or educate ourselves out of this domination system. The church has to embody a new way of being that centers on compassion and human equality. With creativity and imagination, the church must join with others in mobilizing to reclaim the nondominating power that transforms society. The direction I see for the future is towards locally owned and managed economies that rely largely on local resources that meet the needs of the community and maintain balance with the environment. We will need new forms of social organization, perhaps more like cells of a living organism, which are in constant and mutually supportive interaction with each other, while maintaining their individual integrity and functioning together as part of a larger whole.

I am convinced that only deep movements of faith and justice can hope to redirect this nation, which is so deeply divided over race, crippled by economic exploitation, far down the track of an awful war, and engaged in fierce self-delusion about its place in the world. The price we and the world pay for this hubris is so high. People of faith must rise to the task. Even as things stand, healing will be generations down the road. Yet I believe there are other possibilities for us as a nation. And if I am wrong, I will still do this work, because it is my deepest calling, and informs everything I do.

***

"I am reminded of the sincere faith that lived first in your grandmother," the apostle Paul is portrayed writing to Timothy. "So rekindle the gift of God that is within you through the laying on of my hands; for God did not give us a spirit of cowardice, but rather a spirit of power, love and

---

tions, has worked closely with Nelson on numerous educational projects. See also Marsh (2005). On Dr. King's interest in meeting with Merton, see volume I, chapter 2, n. 18 and sources cited there; on the Memphis living wage struggle that ultimately got King killed by his government see volume I, Introduction, n. 5 and references.

discipline" (2 Tim 1:5-7). We thought of this when Nelson answered our question about where his courage and conviction come from. He looked us straight in the eye and said, "I was born in 1943. Many of the people who held me in their hands had been slaves or were the children of slaves. I do this work because I need to bear witness to that." Maya Angelou is right: "History, despite its wrenching pain, cannot be unlived."

Nelson Johnson echoes Ezekiel's searing indictment of a society in denial of its own contradictions:

> Because, in truth, they have misled my people, saying, "Peace!" when there is no peace; and because, when the people build a wall, these prophets smear whitewash on it . . . I the Lord will break down the wall that you have smeared with whitewash, and bring it to the ground, so that its foundation will be laid bare. (Ezek 13:10, 14)

Yet this "laying bare" led Nelson and his colleagues to a historic truth and reconciliation process that holds the possibility of healing for both victims and perpetrators of deeply rooted historical injustices.

This same Ezekiel, in his famous vision of the valley of dry bones, was asked by Yahweh, "Mortal, can these bones live?" (Ezek 37:3). Mennonite pastor and Cheyenne peace chief Lawrence Hart's work in repatriation embodies the hope of God's answer to that difficult question of the dismembered past: "I will bring you up from your graves, O my people, and bring you back to your land" (37:12).

With a moral authority forged through excruciating oppression, Nelson and Lawrence, with Wendy Rose, "will not let us forget." And with a moral vision shaped by deep gospel and cultural commitments, they have become elder statesmen of reconciliation. By heeding their wisdom and learning from their experiments in truth, Angelou's promise will also be realized: If faced with courage, this painful history will not be lived again.

CONCLUSION

In the poem that stands as an epigraph to this volume, "While Love Is Unfashionable," Alice Walker bids us to "live unfashionably," to "be poor in all but truth, and courage," and to "gather blossoms under fire."[1] In volume I we invoked Irish poet Seamus Heaney's vision:

> The longed-for tidal wave
> Of justice can rise up,
> And hope and history rhyme.
> So hope for a great sea-change
> On the far side of revenge.

We think these verses from very different bards poignantly articulate a common spiritual longing for, and earnest invitation to, the work of restorative justice and peacemaking in a history captive to the curse of Lamech: the spiral of violence and retribution.

To take up this call, as the author of Ephesians put it two millennia ago, we must "put on the *whole* armor of God" (Eph 6:11).[2] This ancient exhortation motivated us to search, in part 1 of this volume, for characteristics of a holistic and ecumenical approach to restorative justice and peacemaking. The times demand nothing less than a full spectrum of strategies (chapter 2), which pay critical attention to the genesis of violence (chapter 1) and to the dynamics of power and privilege (chapter 3).

The divine vocation to become "ambassadors of reconciliation" (2 Cor 5:19f.), in turn, animated conversations in part 2 with nine colleagues in

---

1. In November 2008 Walker wrote that the poem came "out of the love I felt for my own non-black husband, a good man I married in 1967, a time when our marriage was illegal in the American South where I was born" (posted at http://alicewalkersblog.blogspot .com/2008/11/marrying-good-men.html). Jaggi (2005) writes that Walker's "marriage came under pressure, not only from the Ku Klux Klan but from black nationalists, who saw her husband as an interloper.... A fictional memoir of her marriage in *The Way Forward Is with a Broken Heart* (2000) traced the end of an idealism that 'our love made us bulletproof.'" Walker recently recited the poem at a marriage ceremony of two "good white men" at which she presided, mindful of the equally "unfashionable" nature of their union. She assured the couple, however, that they were in "the safest place of all: a place where love and freedom were honored" (posted at ibid.).

2. See volume I, 4E.

faith and practice who, in our opinion, are broadening and deepening the meaning of restorative justice and peacemaking today. Their lived testimonies, individually and together, make it difficult to dismiss the biblical vision as hopelessly idealistic. Yet ultimately the proper response to the inspiration of their work is *conspiracy*—"breathing together" new experiments in personal and political transformation.

We hope that the biblical, analytical, and biographical material offered in the two volumes of this project will help to widen the horizon of possibility for such conspiracies, however unfashionable they may seem. May we Christians embrace a discipleship that "gathers blossoms under fire" in order to forge a "sea-change on the far side of revenge."

APPENDIX

Restorative Justice Principles in the Greensboro Truth and Community Reconciliation Project

Swearing in of GTCRP Commissioners.
Photo credit: Elliot Fratkin, Greensboro Justice Fund, used with permission

We have argued in this book that truth and reconciliation work is an important contemporary expression of restorative justice that addresses historic, collective trauma (above, 2C). While the process in South Africa after the fall of the apartheid regime is the best known, TRCs have taken place in many other countries in the last two decades (see Daye, 2004). Here we want to underscore our contention by examining more closely how a TRC process applies principles of restorative justice as defined in victim-offender facilitation work. We will take the example of the Greensboro Truth and Community Reconciliation Project profiled above (7B)—the first time this process has come to the United States—with which we had the privilege of being involved.

Many of the ideas in this appendix were presented by Elaine to the Greensboro Truth and Community Reconciliation Project at the twenty-fourth commemoration of the massacre on November 1, 2003. They have been significantly edited and expanded in light of the May 2006 Greensboro Truth and Reconciliation Commission report.

Restorative justice attempts to respond to crime and violation in order to find an alternative to punishment, further alienation, and shame. The process is driven by the needs of the victim or survivor and their community, and holds offenders accountable for harm caused. Through practices of recognizing injustices and needs, making reparations, and recovenanting, restorative justice provides an opportunity for restoration, healing, and even forgiveness.

The criminal justice system defines crime exclusively as a violation of the law; the State is the victim and the truth is reduced to the facts of the case. Neither the social relationship between victim and offender, nor the deeper meaning of the events is addressed (see above, 4A, i). This approach to justice clearly did not work in the wake of the 1979 Massacre in Greensboro; three trials brought neither justice, closure, nor understanding.

In contrast, restorative justice sees crime as fundamentally relational: people violate people, and these social relationships must be repaired in order for "justice" to be achieved. The three questions that guide restorative justice in interpersonal facilitation between victims and offenders are:

- Who was harmed?
- What are the needs of those who were harmed?
- Who is responsible to meet these needs?

The Greensboro Truth and Community Reconciliation Project (GTCRP) attempted to address each of these questions in the case of the politically motivated violence of the November 3 Massacre (summarized above, 7B, i).

Those harmed by these events were not only the five people killed and ten people wounded and their family and friends; an entire community was traumatized by this eruption of race and class violence, which was then exacerbated by denial and cover-up by city officials and the dominant media. Assessing both the needs of the various parties harmed in Greensboro and how to address those needs is, therefore, complex but crucial.

Victim-offender facilitation has developed the following working list of needs and responsibilities of victims, offenders, and their respective communities (see Toews, 2006: 25ff.). We list these here and show how they apply to the GTCRP:

Some Needs of Victims and Their Families

1. *Physical and emotional safety.* Prior to the GTCRP, neither physical nor emotional safety had been secured for the survivors of the massacre, who were maligned, marginalized, and harassed by police. In

the absence of criminal convictions or civic acknowledgment, the atmosphere of fear and uncertainty remained, and the subject of 1979 was studiously avoided in public discourse. The job of the GTCRP was to change this climate through a public examination of this legacy, in order to drain it of its toxic power to silence.

2. *Supportive relationships.* As survivor Nelson Johnson points out (above, 7B, ii), he was profoundly isolated as a result of the media and political "management" of the events of 1979. The GTCRP offered him and other survivors the solidarity, social recognition, and support of those parts of the wider community who were willing to face this legacy honestly.

3. *Empowerment.* Survivors experienced job loss and social stigma in the wake of 1979. While the GTCRP didn't offer reparation for past economic losses or physical injuries, it helped heal the psychic wounds of marginalization. It also challenged the community, through its education and advocacy, to work toward the structural changes that can prevent racist violence in the future (see below).

4. *Information, answers, and meaning.* Victims of crime typically ask:

- What happened, and why did it happen to me?
- Why did I act the way I did at the time?
- What has happened with the case?
- Why have I acted as I have since the crime?
- What if it happens again?
- What does this mean for me and for my outlook (my faith, my vision of the world, my future)?

Here we see interesting differences between the experience of crime and politically motivated violence. The victim of a carjacking, who perceives crime as random, may well wonder why *she* was attacked. Victims of political violence, on the other hand, almost always know *exactly* why attacks happened, and why *they* were targeted. Their problem is that the *public* is not clear about (or refuses to acknowledge) the political motivations and injustices involved, thus isolating the victims further.[1]

In the case of the November 3, 1979, labor rally, the organizers had already skirmished with their political opponents over their efforts to name race and class injustices in the local textile mills and to call out the Klan's culpability. Indeed, organizers knew there might be an attack on their march, but were forced to rely on police

---

1. In situations of systemic oppression, the community as a whole understands the reasons for its marginalization, even though individuals (particularly children) may not comprehend the discrimination.

protection since a condition for their parade permit was that they could not carry weapons. The commission's findings made it clear that not only did the police fail to provide this protection, but also they were complicit in the planning and execution of the violence.

In the aftermath of the events, the survivors understood that the criminal prosecution of the case was thoroughly political, and the third of three separate trials brought only a slim margin of justice. The massacre, then, didn't so much *change* their outlook on society (as street crime often does for victims) as *deepen* their political convictions about social injustice. That said, the trauma compelled some survivors toward a spiritual turn (notably Rev. Johnson; above, 7B, ii).

5. *Their story heard and vindicated, and an opportunity to express their feelings to the offender.* While survivors of political violence may, like a victim of street crime, wish to face the perpetrator(s), the greater need is to have their story and perspective understood and vindicated by the public. Typically, the narrative of the events in question has been distorted or suppressed by those in power. The resulting gap between the survivor's experiences and the dominant culture's perceptions feeds the former's cognitive dissonance and rage, and maintains the latter's illusion of "innocence."

For example, every time the events of 1979 were described in the Greensboro media or by City Hall apologists as a "shootout between extremist groups," the survivors experienced revictimization and continuing frustration. This is why the "truth" part of TRC processes is so crucial. Only by "setting the record straight" can the suffering endured by victims of oppression be given meaning. But "public understanding" can be a long-term educational project. As Rev. Johnson points out, one cannot properly interpret the massacre without taking into account the historical matrix of race and class oppression in the mid-South. In this sense, the work of the GTCRP is necessary but not sufficient; the long-term goal is to transform the "bigger story" of race and labor relations.

6. *Compensation for losses.* In all cases of lethal violation, reparation can only be symbolic. While TRC processes do not rule out forms of material compensation, these are often difficult to determine and procure. In the Greensboro Truth Commission, survivors' losses, which had been compounded by a quarter century of public obfuscation, were finally given visibility and acknowledgment. Moreover, the commission recommended that those involved in the shootings should offer restitution to the victims in the form of contributions in their names to a public monument commemorating this tragedy or to organizations involved in social justice work.

7. *Remorse from offender, commitment not to repeat offense.* One of the gifts of the Greensboro process was a meeting in which one of the primary shooters—local former Nazi leader Roland Wood— expressed remorse to commissioners and to survivor Signe Waller, the spouse of one of those killed. It was a healing moment for Waller, who said afterward: "It was a very emotional conversation, but at the end I was so filled with hope. He was remorseful, he apologized. He begged for my forgiveness. And I realized that if this man—who in 1979 was a thug, a racist, a man full of hate— could genuinely change, then I know there is hope for this entire world. Every thug, every racist, every imperialist president, *everyone* can be transformed. *I* have been transformed, and I think if our five comrades were alive today, they would be transformed."[2]

8. *Transcending/surviving the trauma.* The victims of the 1979 Massacre moved from being "survivors" to "healers" by taking the initiative to organize the GTCRP. Rev. Johnson understood that this process was needed to complete his own transaction of the events, but also, and more importantly, for the health of the wider Greensboro community.

9. *Relief for victim's family—from their own suffering and/or from the burden of caretaking the victim's trauma.* In Greensboro, the events had profound impact on the children of the victims. Now adults, they received a measure of relief through the GTCRP. The commission recommended that religious leadership should plan and facilitate a healing retreat for children of both victims and offenders.

Restorative justice acknowledges that the offender is also harmed by their violating actions, and that is certainly the case with those who did the conspiring and shooting in 1979. The list of needs thus continues:

Some Needs of Offenders and Their Families

1. *Physical and emotional safety from retaliation (in prison and on the street).* None of the perpetrators or conspirators behind the 1979 Massacre ever went to jail. In the course of the GTCRP, however, a son of one of the shooters privately contacted Rev. Johnson (above, 7B, ii), expressing his fear of job loss and of retaliation if he were to come forward—not from the survivors, but from his Klan associates! Clearly, then, at least some offenders and their families did not feel safe to break the conspiracy of silence after the shootings.

---

2. Interview appears in the film *Greensboro: Closer to the Truth* by Adam Zucker (Longnook Pictures, 2007).

2. *Supportive relationships.* The GTCRP attempted to create a safe environment for offenders as well, though as noted only one shooter came forward to express his remorse publicly. Rev. Johnson had significant off-the-record pastoral conversations with a couple of adult children of the perpetrators, and personally reached out to Klan members at commission meetings.

3. *Information about legal proceedings, options, including restorative justice.* The GTCRP carried no threat of further prosecution for the perpetrators and began their outreach in 2002 explaining their restorative intent. It was an uphill battle given the dominant culture's commitment to retribution.

4. *Accountability:*

   - Admit one's choice to commit the crime.
   - Understand the human consequences of the crime.
   - Address harms, take opportunity to make things right.
   - Face the victim, if possible and appropriate.

   Restorative justice depends on perpetrators acknowledging their culpability and taking responsibility for their offense. The Greensboro Commission was handicapped by the fact that they did not have this baseline. Significant numbers of Klan and Nazis attended the commission hearings, and a few testified but were unrepentant. Only Roland Wood admitted his guilt on record and asked for forgiveness. Though the commission found the Greensboro Police Department was both negligent and complicit in the events of 1979, no official recognition or apology was forthcoming.

5. *Storytelling (past and present).* The commission offered Klan members, Nazis, and police officers opportunities to tell their side of the story. Much of their testimony simply reiterated previous assertions of innocence—and in some cases repeated vengeful comments. Because the commission did not hold the power of prosecution (as did the South Africa Commission), it was unable to apply legal pressure on perpetrators to own up to their roles. Whether racist rants or false assertions should be allowed to stand unchallenged in grassroots TRC processes is a vigorous point of debate in the field.

6. *Understand why one committed the crime, transforming identity:*

   - Healing from past harms and violations.
   - Treatment of addictions.
   - Opportunities to improve work skills, education, and personal competencies.
   - Empowerment to integrate into community.
   - Grace.

The hope for offenders in a restorative justice process is that they will embrace the difficult journey of self- and social awareness and transformation. The problem with political violence—particularly if it has been ignored or exonerated in criminal court, as was the case in Greensboro—is that unless and until there is public disapproval (even shaming) for such attacks, there is little social or moral incentive for the perpetrators to change. We do not know if those involved in the 1979 shooting have, as a result of the GTCRP, begun privately to question their ideology, loyalties, and culpability. The commission's work to change community attitudes in Greensboro, however, as an expression of public grace, may make it more possible for the offenders to take responsibility for their actions in the future.

7. *Support for imprisoned offender's family*:

- Opportunity for family to make amends on loved ones' behalf.
- Family services (e.g., to help them cope with the loss of offender's income).
- Prison visitation and transportation services.
- Transition help when offender comes home.

Though offender incarceration was not an issue in Greensboro, the GTCRP was ready to help perpetrators and their families had they come forward. In order for offenders to change, however, their social networks must be transformed. The whole community must discover ways to wean persons from participating in racist gangs, and this cannot be done without also addressing social issues such as employment, education, and welfare. This brings us to the final set of questions.

Some Needs of Community

The third pillar of restorative justice is to address the needs of the community (church, neighborhood, school, and so on) impacted by a crime. These concerns include:

- Safety: decreased recidivism, crime, and fear.
- Community service by offender.
- Reintegrating victim and offender back into community, with structures for the accountability and welfare of both.
- Education.

In conclusion to their two-year investigation, which included public and private hearings, the Greensboro Truth and Community Reconciliation

Commission issued a 529-page report on May 25, 2006 (available at www
.greensborotrc.org). Their findings and conclusions were followed by a set of
recommendations, which address many of the above community concerns.

Commission recommendations to the community of Greensboro,
which were discussed in a series of forums in the year following the report,
fell into four categories:

1. *Acknowledgment*, including "steps to recognize rights and responsibilities and acknowledge that wrongs were committed and harms
   occurred." These included:

   - The city should formally incorporate the events of November 3
     into its history and make a proclamation that highlights their
     importance.
   - The Greensboro Police Department and City of Greensboro
     should issue public apologies for their failure to protect the
     public (specifically demonstrators and residents of the neigh-
     borhood where the shooting took place).
   - Local museums should develop an exhibit commemorating the
     tragic shootings.
   - A public monument should be built on the site of the shootings
     to honor those killed and wounded.

2. *Institutional reform*, to prevent future abuses. These included:

   - All city and county employees and their subcontractors should
     be paid a living wage.
   - All city and county employees should engage in antiracism
     training.
   - The city should issue annual reports on race relations and racial
     disparities.
   - A citizens' committee should be established by the Human
     Relations Commission to create both a temporary and perma-
     nent police review board.
   - Guilford County should increase funding to serve low-income
     residents.
   - County schools should create curriculum based on the events
     of November 3 for use in public schools.
   - Citizens and city officials should create a community justice
     center to address the low levels of trust among people of color
     and poor people in the criminal justice system, and to promote
     restorative justice.
   - The Greensboro *News & Record* should work with other media
     outlets to host a citywide citizens' group that would give feed-
     back on news process, content, quality, and ethics.

3. *Criminal justice and civil remedies.* The commission supported the ongoing investigation into corruption in the Greensboro Police Department, and noted that commissioners and staff had also been illegally surveilled. It also supported either criminal prosecution or civil action against illegal acts by city agents, in order to restore public trust.

4. *Citizen transformation and engagement.* The commission urged individual citizens to commit to understanding issues of racism, poverty, oppression, privilege, and justice, and to engage in antiracism training and diversity education.

Regardless of the degree to which its recommendations are implemented in the future, we believe the Greensboro Commission did a exemplary job of mapping the issues germane to community transformation. And it did so despite considerable public and covert opposition, including death threats. As their report states:

> As the GTRC met with surveillance, intimidation and rumor-mongering at the institutional level, at the personal level we found indifference, fear and resistance. The mayor once commented to us that he found it "unappetizing" to engage in a process that speaks openly about issues of poverty, labor, capital, race and hate. It appears that many in our community share his distaste. (Executive Summary, p. 25)

The commission's work thus provides a model of restorative justice applied to issues of historic violation and systemic inequality.

To summarize, the GTCRP and the commission embodied many of the practices of restorative justice we have identified in this book:

- It dared to analyze how social power is distributed in the community and to address structural issues, understanding that these lay at the roots of violence (above, chapter 3).
- It examined the chronic places of violence in the community and why these conditions persist (above, chapter 1).
- It called for accountability from perpetrating persons and institutions, including the difficult and contentious concerns around police complicity, media misrepresentation, and political silencing.
- It provided a safe space for victims, offenders, and their families and community members to tell their story and to listen to others.
- It pioneered a process of historical revisitation, truth-telling, and the power of testimony. Public processing of pain is difficult, and we North Americans and our governments do not do it well—yet

all of the memorials around the events of September 11, 2001, attest to the importance of cathartic memory.

- It offered public acknowledgment of people's pain, enabling all parties to move *past* trauma by moving *through* it.
- It called for a measure of reparation, if primarily through public monuments and revising "official" city history—and as we saw in the witness of Elder Lawrence Hart (above, 7A, ii), such acknowledgments are crucial for healing the past.
- It attempted to outline what community "recovenanting" might look like, with all sectors of Greensboro urged to take responsibility for the past and the future.
- Most importantly, it called for concrete political and structural change. Rev. Johnson rightly insists that exercises in historical truth-telling must lead to real social change in order to fulfill their purpose. The civil rights movement would not have meant as much, he points out, if it had not ultimately led to the overturning of segregation laws.

Our national history is riddled with unresolved historic injustices, from the Middle Passage to the My Lai Massacre, from the Salem witch trials to Wounded Knee. Indeed, untransacted public trauma is an old and persistent strand in the human story, as unhealed collective wounds are passed down from generation to generation. In the Hebrew Bible this is referred to as "visiting the sins of the parents on the children." Yet Israel's prophets warned against the people's temptation to remain captive to their violent or duplicitous past, taking shadowy refuge in resignation or despair. As Ezekiel put it, "What do you mean by repeating this proverb concerning our land: 'The fathers have eaten sour grapes and the children's teeth are set on edge?' As I live, says the Lord, this proverb shall no more be used by you in Israel" (Ezek 18:2; cf. Jer 31:29f).

The vocation of faith is to envision a future that is ever mindful of, but healed from, the sins of the past. It is to forge justice without retribution and to find liberation from the long-term consequences of violation. Whether addressing crime, historic trauma, or systemic oppression, the work of restorative justice requires moral imagination and political courage. In 1960, when the four young men sat down at a segregated Greensboro Woolworth's lunch counter, they ignited a nonviolent revolution in America. The Greensboro Truth and Community Reconciliation Project has fanned that flame back to life again.

REFERENCES

Aldridge, Robert C.
  1989   *Nuclear Empire*. Vancouver: New Star Books.
Angelou, Maya.
  1993   *On the Pulse of Morning*. New York: Random House.
Arendt, Hannah.
  1998   *The Human Condition*. Chicago: University of Chicago Press.
Avruch, Kevin, and Beatriz Vejarano
  2002   "Truth and Reconciliation Commissions: A Review Essay and Anno-
          tated Bibliography." *The Online Journal of Peace and Conflict Resolution*
          4/2 (Spring).
Baldus, David, George Woodworth, and Charles A. Pulaski.
  1990   *Equal Justice and the Death Penalty: A Legal and Empirical Analysis*.
          Hanover, NH: University Press of New England.
Barnett, Erica.
  1999   *Marietta Jaeger: Crusader against Capital Punishment*. Evanston, IL:
          John Gordon Burke Publisher, Inc.
Bender, Harold S.
  1944   *The Anabaptist Vision*. Scottdale, PA: Herald Press.
Berger, Peter L., and Thomas Luckmann.
  1966   *The Social Construction of Reality: A Treatise in the Sociology of Knowl-
          edge*. New York: Doubleday.
Bermanzohn, Sally A.
  2003   *Through Survivors' Eyes: From the Sixties to the Greensboro Massacre*.
          Nashville: Vanderbilt University Press.
Berrigan, Daniel, S.J.
  2004   *The Trial of the Catonsville Nine*. New York: Fordham University
          Press.
Berrigan, Philip.
  1978   *Of Beasts and Beastly Images: Essays under the BOMB*. Baltimore: Fort-
          kamp.
Berrigan, Philip, and Elizabeth McAlister.
  1989   *The Time's Discipline: The Beatitudes and Nuclear Resistance*. Portland:
          Sunburst Press.
Berrigan, Philip, and Fred Wilcox.
  1996   *Fighting the Lamb's War: Skirmishes with the American Empire. The Auto-
          biography of Philip Berrigan*. Monroe, ME: Common Courage Press.

Bondurant, Joan.
  1971   *Conquest of Violence: The Gandhian Philosophy of Conflict.* Revised edition. Berkeley: University of California Press.
Branch, Taylor.
  2006   *At Canaan's Edge: America in the King Years (1965-68).* New York: Simon & Schuster.
  1998   *Pillar of Fire: America in the King Years (1963-65).* New York: Simon & Schuster.
  1988   *Parting the Waters: America in the King Years (1954-63).* New York: Simon & Schuster.
Brinton, Daniel Garrison, and Constantine Samuel Rafinesque.
  1885   *The Lenâpé and Their Legends: With the Complete Text and Symbols of the Walam Olum, a New Translation, and an Inquiry into Its Authenticity.* Published by D.G. Brinton.
Brown, Tricia Gates, ed.
  2008   *118 Days: Christian Peacemakers Teams Held Hostage in Iraq.* Telford, PA: Cascadia Publishing House/Christian Peacemakers Teams.
  2005   *Getting in the Way: Stories from Christian Peacemaker Teams.* Scottdale, PA: Herald Press.
Bush, Robert A. Baruch, and Joseph P. Folger.
  1994   *The Promise of Mediation: Responding to Conflict through Empowerment and Recognition.* San Francisco: Jossey-Bass Publishers.
Camara, Dom Helder.
  1971   *Spiral of Violence.* New York: Continuum International.
Carter, Jimmy.
  2006   *Palestine: Peace Not Apartheid.* New York: Simon and Schuster.
Cayley, David.
  1998   *The Expanding Prison: The Crisis in Crime and Punishment and the Search for Alternatives.* Cleveland: Pilgrim Press.
Chafe, William Henry.
  1981   *Civilities and Civil Rights: Greensboro, North Carolina, and the Black Struggle for Freedom.* New York: Oxford University Press US.
Chakrabarti, Mohit.
  2000   *The Gandhian Philosophy of Spinning-Wheel.* New Delhi: Concept Publishing Company.
Chomsky, Noam.
  2001   *9-11.* Open Media Publishing. New York: Seven Stories Press.
Cichon, Ted.
  2000   "The Corrymeela Community: 'The Hill of Hope' or an Illusion?" *The Online Journal of Peace and Conflict Resolution* 3/3 (Fall).
Clark, Ramsey.
  1970   *Crime in America: Observations on Its Nature, Causes, Prevention, and Control.* New York: Simon and Schuster.
Cole, Susan, and Hal Taussig.
  2004   "Jesus and Sophia." In *The Wisdom of Daughters: Two Decades of the*

Voice of Christian Feminism, edited by Reta Halteman Finger and Kari Sandhaas. Minneapolis: Augsburg Books.

Colson, Charles, and Mark Earley.
2003   *Six Million Angels: Stories from 20 years of Angel Tree's Ministry to the Children of Prisoners.* Ann Arbor: Servant Publications.

Consedine, Jim.
1999   *Restorative Justice: Healing the Effects of Crime.* Harrisonburg, VA: Ploughshares Publications.

Consedine, Jim, and Helen Bowen.
1999   *Restorative Justice: Contemporary Themes and Practice.* Harrisonburg, VA: Ploughshares Publications.

Cooney, Robert, and Helen Michalowski, eds.
1987   *The Power of the People: Active Nonviolence in the United States.* Washington, DC: Peace Press.

Cose, Ellis.
2004   *Bone to Pick: Of Forgiveness, Reconciliation, Reparation, and Revenge.* New York: Simon and Schuster.

Crocker, Chester A., Fen Osler Hampson, and Pamela R. Aall, eds.
2007   *Leashing the Dogs of War: Conflict Management in a Divided World.* Washington, DC: U.S. Institute of Peace Press.

Crossan, John Dominic.
1999   *Birth of Christianity: Discovering What Happened in the Years Immediately after the Execution of Jesus.* New York: Continuum.

Crowe, Ann H.
2000   *Jurisdictional Technical Assistance Package for Juvenile Corrections.* Washington, DC: U.S. Department of Justice, Office of Juvenile Justice and Delinquency Prevention.

Daniel, Donald, and Bradd Hayes, eds.
1995   *Beyond Traditional Peacekeeping.* New York: Macmillan.

Davis, Murphy.
1985   "Faith in the Unseen Realities." *Sojourners Magazine* (June).

Daye, Russell.
2004   *Political Forgiveness: Lessons from South Africa.* Maryknoll, NY: Orbis Books.

de Leon-Hartshorne, Iris, Tobin Miller Shearer, and Regina Shands Stoltzfus.
2001   *Set Free: A Journey toward Solidarity against Racism.* Scottdale, PA: Herald Press.

De Veaux, Alexis.
2004   *Warrior Poet: A Biography of Audre Lorde.* New York: W. W. Norton & Company.

Dickson-Gilmore, Jane, and Carol La Prairie
2005   *"Will the Circle be Unbroken?" Aboriginal Communities, Restorative Justice, and the Challenges of Conflict and Change.* Toronto: University of Toronto Press.

Douglass, James W.
  2008 *JFK and the Unspeakable: Why He Died and Why It Matters*. Maryknoll,
         NY: Orbis Books.
Dugan, Maire.
  1996 "A Nested Theory of Conflict." *A Leadership Journal: Women in Lead-
         ership—Sharing the Vision* 1/1 (July), pp. 9-20.
Enright, Robert D., and Joanna North, eds.
  1998 *Exploring Forgiveness*. Madison: University of Wisconsin Press.
Enns, Elaine, and Ched Myers.
  1999 "Power, Gender and Conflict." In *Making Peace with Conflict: Practi-
         cal Skills for Conflict Transformation*, edited by Carolyn Schrock-Shenk
         and Lawrence Ressler. Scottdale, PA: Herald Press.
Estep, William.
  1996 *The Anabaptist Story: An Introduction to Sixteenth-Century Anabaptism*.
         Third revised edition. Grand Rapids: Eerdmans Publishing.
Ferrell, Claudine L.
  2006 *The Abolitionist Movement*. Abingdon, UK: Greenwood Publishing
         Group.
Fisas Armengol, Vicenç.
  1995 *Blue Geopolitics: The United Nations Reform and the Future of the Blue
         Helmets*. Hanover, NH: University Press of New England.
Fisher, Roger, William Ury, and Bruce Patton.
  1991 *Getting to Yes: Negotiating Agreement without Giving In*. Boston:
         Houghton Mifflin Harcourt.
Flanagan, Sabina.
  1998 *Hildegard of Bingen, 1098-1179: A Visionary Life*. New York: Rout-
         ledge.
Foley, Michael S.
  2003 *Confronting the War Machine: Draft Resistance during the Vietnam War*.
         Chapel Hill: University of North Carolina Press.
Foner, Eric.
  2002 *Reconstruction: America's Unfinished Revolution, 1863-1877*. New York:
         HarperCollins.
Fortune, Marie M., and Joretta L. Marshall.
  2004 *Forgiveness and Abuse: Jewish and Christian Reflections*. Philadelphia:
         Haworth Press.
Gandhi, Mohandas Karamchand.
  1954 *Gandhi's Autobiography: The Story of My Experiments with Truth*. Jack-
         son, TN: Public Affairs Books.
Gathje, Peter R.
  2006 "Sharing the Bread of Life: Hospitality and Resistance at the Open
         Door Community." Atlanta: Open Door Publications.
  2002 *A Work of Hospitality: The Open Door Reader, 1982-2002*. Atlanta: Open
         Door Publications.
  1991 *Christ Comes in the Stranger's Guise: A History of the Open Door Com-
         munity*. Atlanta: Open Door Publications.

Gilligan, James.
    1997   *Violence: Reflections on a National Epidemic.* New York: Vintage Books.
Gort Jerald D., Henry Jansen, Hendrik M. Vroom, eds.
    2002   Religion, Conflict and Reconciliation: Multifaith Ideals and Realities. New York: Rodopi.
Grandin, Greg, and Thomas Miller Klubock.
    2007   *Truth Commissions: State Terror, History, and Memory.* Durham, NC: Duke University Press.
Greensboro Truth and Reconciliation Commission.
    2006   *Commission Report, Executive Summary.* Greensboro, North Carolina.
Griffin, David Ray.
    2006   *9/11 and American Empire: Intellectuals Speak Out.* Ithaca: Olive Branch Press.
Hammarskjold, Dag.
    1964   *Markings,* translated by Leif Sjoberg and W. H. Auden. New York: Random House.
Hatch, Thom.
    2004   *Black Kettle: The Cheyenne Chief Who Sought Peace but Found War.* Hoboken, NJ: Wiley Publishing.
Harding, Vincent.
    2008   *Martin Luther King: The Inconvenient Hero.* Second edition. Maryknoll, NY: Orbis Books.
    1990   *Hope and History: Why We Must Share the Story of the Movement.* Maryknoll, NY: Orbis Books.
Hersh, Seymour M.
    2004   *Chain of Command: The Road from 9/11 to Abu Ghraib.* New York: HarperCollins.
Hinz-Penner, Raylene.
    2007   *Searching for Sacred Ground: The Journey of Chief Lawrence Hart, Mennonite.* Telford, PA: Cascadia Publishing.
Hogan, Wesley C.
    2007   *Many Minds, One Heart: SNCC's Dream for a New America.* Chapel Hill: University of North Carolina Press.
Hoig, Stan.
    1980   *The Peace Chiefs of the Cheyennes.* Norman: University of Oklahoma Press.
Hollyday, Joyce.
    1994   *Clothed with the Sun: Biblical Women, Social Justice and Us.* Louisville: Westminster/John Knox Press.
Honey, Michael Keith.
    1999   *Black Workers Remember: An Oral History of Segregation, Unionism, and the Freedom Struggle.* Berkeley: University of California Press.
hooks, bell.
    2000   *Where We Stand: Class Matters.* New York: Routledge.
Jaeger, Marietta.
    1983   *The Lost Child.* Grand Rapids: Zondervan.

Jaggi, Maya.
    2005   "Redemption Songs." *The Guardian* (UK), Saturday, January 15, Fea-
            tures & Reviews, p. 20.
Jeffries, John Calvin.
    2001   *Justice Lewis F. Powell, Jr.* New York: Fordham University Press.
Johnson, Allan G.
    2005   *The Gender Knot: Unraveling Our Patriarchal Legacy.* Philadelphia:
            Temple University Press.
Johnstone, Gerry.
    2002   *Restorative Justice: Ideas, Values, Debates.* Portland: Willan.
Juergensmeyer, Mark.
    1984   *Fighting with Gandhi.* San Francisco: Harper & Row.
Judah, Eleanor Hannon, and Michael Bryant, eds.
    2004   *Criminal Justice: Retribution vs. Restoration.* Philadelphia: Haworth
            Press.
Keer, Dhananjay.
    1973   *Mahatma Gandhi: Political Saint and Unarmed Prophet.* New Dehli:
            Suruchi Prakashan.
Kellermann, Bill Wylie.
    1991   *Seasons of Faith and Conscience: Kairos, Confession, Liturgy.* Maryknoll,
            NY: Orbis Books.
Kern, Kathleen.
    2008   *In Harm's Way: A History of Christian Peacemaker Teams.* Telford, PA:
            Cascadia Press.
Kim, Sebastian, Pauline Kollontai, and Greg Hoyland, eds.
    2008   *Peace and Reconciliation: In Search of Shared Identity.* Surrey, UK: Ash-
            gate Publishing Group, Ltd.
King, Martin Luther, Jr.
    1967   *Where Do We Go From Here? Chaos or Community?* New York: Harper
            & Row.
King, Rachel.
    2003   *Don't Kill in Our Names: Families of Murder Victims Speak Out against
            the Death Penalty.* Piscataway, NJ: Rutgers University Press.
Klaiber, Jeffrey.
    1998   *The Church, Dictatorships, and Democracy in Latin America.* Maryknoll,
            NY: Orbis Books.
Kovic, Christine
    2003   "The Struggle for Liberation and Reconciliation in Chiapas, Mexico:
            Las Abejas and the Path of Nonviolent Resistance." *Latin American
            Perspectives* 30/3:58-79.
Kritek, Phyllis Beck.
    1994   *Negotiating at an Uneven Table: A Practical Approach to Working with
            Difference and Diversity.* San Francisco: Jossey-Bass Publishers.
Laffin, Arthur, ed.
    2003   *Swords into Plowshares: A Chronology of Plowshares Disarmament Actions,
            1980-2003.* Revised edition. New York: Rose Hill Books.

Langer, Susanne K.
1957   *Philosophy in a New Key: A Study in the Symbolism of Reason, Rite, and Art.* Cambridge, MA: Harvard University Press.
Larson, Kate Clifford.
2007   *Bound for the Promised Land: Harriet Tubman: Portrait of an American Hero.* New York: Ballantine Books.
Lederach, John Paul.
2003   *The Little Book of Conflict Transformation.* Intercourse, PA: Good Books.
1997   *Building Peace: Sustainable Reconciliation in Divided Societies.* Washington, DC: United States Institute of Peace Press.
Lederach, John Paul, and Janice Moomaw Jenner, eds.
2002   *A Handbook of International Peacebuilding: Into the Eye of the Storm.* San Francisco: Jossey-Bass Publications.
Llewellyn, Karl Nickerson, William T. Ross, and Edward Adamson Hoebel.
2002   *The Cheyenne Way: Conflict and Case Law in Primitive Jurisprudence.* Buffalo: Wm. S. Hein & Co. (reissue of 1941 edition).
Lorde, Audre.
2007   *Sister Outsider: Essays and Speeches by Audre Lorde.* Berkeley: Crossing Press.
1996   *Zami: A New Spelling of My Name.* Kitchener, ON: Pandora Press.
1995   *The Cancer Journals.* San Francisco: Aunt Lute Books.
Lynd, Alice, and Staughton Lynd, eds.
1995   *Nonviolence in America: A Documentary History.* Maryknoll, NY: Orbis Books.
MacIntyre, Alasdair.
1985   *After Virtue: A Study in Moral Theory.* London: Duckworth Press.
1989   *Whose Justice? Which Rationality?* South Bend, IN: University of Notre Dame Press.
MacLeod, Jay.
2008   *Ain't No Makin' It: Aspirations and Attainment in a Low-Income Neighborhood.* Third edition. Boulder, CO: Westview Press.
Magarrell, Lisa, and Joya Wesley.
2006   *Learning from Greensboro: Truth and Reconciliation in the United States.* Pennsylvania Studies in Human Rights. Philadelphia: University of Pennsylvania Press.
Marsh, Charles.
2005   *The Beloved Community: How Faith Shapes Social Justice, From the Civil Rights Movement to Today.* New York: Basic Books.
Marshall, Donna Ramsey.
2008   *Women in War and Peace: Grassroots Peacebuilding.* Darby, PA: Diane Publishing Co.
Martin, Michael T., and Marilyn Yaquinto, eds.
2007   *Redress for Historical Injustices in the United States: On Reparations for Slavery, Jim Crow, and Their Legacies.* Durham, NC: Duke University Press.

McAllister, Pam, ed.
 1982   *Reweaving the Web of Life: Feminism and Nonviolence.* Gabriola Is., BC: New Society Publishers.
McCaslin, Wanda.
 2005   *Justice as Healing: Indigenous Ways.* Saskatoon: University of Saskatchewan Native Law Centre, Living Justice Press.
McDonagh, Francis, ed.
 2009   *Dom Helder Camara: Essential Writings.* Maryknoll, NY: Orbis Books.
Merton, Thomas.
 1966   *Raids on the Unspeakable.* New York: New Directions Publishing.
 1965   *Gandhi on Non-violence: Selected Texts.* New York: New Directions Publishing.
Miller, Jerome G.
 1997   *Search and Destroy: African-American Males in the Criminal Justice System.* New York: Cambridge University Press.
Minas, Anne.
 2000   *Gender Basics: Feminist Perspectives on Women and Men.* Belmont, CA: Wadsworth Publishing Co.
Mirsky, Laura.
 n.d.   "Restorative Justice Practices of Native American, First Nation and Other Indigenous People of North America." www.realjustice.org/library/natjust1.html.
Murphy, Roseanne.
 2007   *Martyr of the Amazon: The Life of Sister Dorothy Stang.* Maryknoll, NY: Orbis Books.
Myers, Ched.
 2002   "Word and World: A People's School." *The Clergy Journal,* September, pp. 8ff.
 2001   *The Biblical Vision of Sabbath Economics.* Washington, DC: Tell the Word Press.
 1994   *Who Will Roll Away the Stone? Discipleship Queries for First World Christians.* Maryknoll, NY: Orbis Books.
 1987   "Storming the Gates of Hell: Reflections on Christian Evangelism in Nuclear Security Areas." In *Border Regions of Faith: An Anthology of Religion and Social Change,* edited by Kenneth Aman. Maryknoll, NY: Orbis Books.
Nepstad, Sharon Erickson.
 2008   *Religion and War Resistance in the Plowshares Movement.* New York: Cambridge University Press.
Pears, Angela.
 2004   *Feminist Christian Encounters: The Methods and Strategies of Feminist Informed Christian Theologies.* Surrey, UK: Ashgate Publishing, Ltd.
Perkinson, James W.
 2004   *White Theology: Outing Supremacy in Modernity.* New York: Palgrave-Macmillan.

Pierson, Ruth, ed.
  1987   *Women and Peace: Theoretical, Historical and Practical Perspectives*. New York: Croom Helm/Methuen Inc.
Piletti, Nelson, and Walter Praxedes.
  1997   *Dom Helder Camara: Entre O Poder E a Profecia*. Sao Paulo: Editora Atica.
Polner, Murray, and Jim O'Grady.
  1997   *Disarmed and Dangerous: The Radical Lives and Times of Daniel and Philip Berrigan*. New York: Basic Books.
Potorti, David, ed.
  2003   *September 11th Families for Peaceful Tomorrows: Turning our Grief into Action for Peace*. New York: ADV Books/Akashic Books.
Powers, Roger, and William B. Vogele, eds.
  1997   *Protest, Power, and Change: Encyclopedia of Nonviolence from ACT-UP to Women's Suffrage*. New York: Garland.
Roediger, David R.
  1999   *The Wages of Whiteness: Race and the Making of the American Working Class*. Revised edition. New York: Verso.
Rose, Wendy.
  1992   "For Some, It's a Time of Mourning." In *Without Discovery: A Native Response to Columbus*, edited by Ray González. Seattle: Broken Moon Press.
Rosenburg, Marshall B.
  1999   *Nonviolent Communication: A Language of Compassion*. Encinitas, CA: PuddleDancer Press.
Ross, Rupert.
  1996   *Returning to the Teachings: Exploring Aboriginal Justice*. Toronto: Penguin Books.
Rubinstein, Robert A.
  2008   *Peacekeeping under Fire: Culture and Intervention*. Boulder, CO: Paradigm Publishers.
Rudin, Jonathan.
  2005   "Aboriginal Justice and Restorative Justice." In *New Direction in Restorative Justice: Issues, Practice, Evaluation*, edited by Elizabeth Elliott and Robert M. Gordon. Portland: Willan Publishing.
Schlesinger, Stephen C.
  2003   *Act of Creation: The Founding of the United Nations*. Boulder, CO: Westview Press.
Schrock-Shenk, Carolyn, ed.
  2000   *Mediation and Facilitation Training Manual: Foundations and Skills for Constructive Conflict Transformation*. Fourth edition. Akron, PA: Mennonite Conciliation Services.
Schrock-Shenk, Carolyn, and Lawrence Ressler, eds.
  1999   *Making Peace with Conflict: Practical Skills for Conflict Transformation*. Scottdale, PA: Herald Press.

Schüssler Fiorenza, Elisabeth.
    1995   *Jesus, Miriam's Child, Sophia's Prophet: Critical Issues in Feminist Christology*. London: SCM Press.

Sharp, Gene.
    1985   *National Security through Civilian-based Defense*. Omaha, NE: Association for Trans Armament Studies.
    1973   *The Politics of Nonviolent Action*. 3 vols. Part One: *Power and Struggle*. Part Two: *The Methods of Nonviolent Action*. Part Three: *The Dynamics of Nonviolent Action*. Boston: Porter Sargent.

Singleton, Glenn, and Curtis Linton.
    2006   *Courageous Conversations about Race: A Field Guide for Achieving Equity in Schools*. Thousand Oaks, CA: Corwin Press.

Stanton, Mary.
    2000   *Selma to Sorrow: The Life and Death of Viola Liuzzo*. Athens: University of Georgia Press.

Tavanti, Marco.
    2002   *Las Abejas: Pacifist Resistance and Syncretic Identities in a Globalizing Chiapas*. Outstanding Dissertations on Religion in History, Society, and Culture. New York: Routledge.

Toews, Barb.
    2006   *The Little Book of Restorative Justice for People in Prisons*. Intercourse, PA: Good Books.

Tutu, Desmond Mpilo.
    1999   *No Future without Forgiveness*. New York: Doubleday.

Tyler, Patrick E.
    2004   "U.N. Chief Ignites Firestorm by Calling Iraq War 'Illegal.'" *New York Times*, September 17.

Tyson, Timothy B.
    2004   *Blood Done Sign My Name*. New York: Three Rivers Press.

Urquhart, Brian.
    1998   *Ralph Bunche: An American Life*. New York: W. W. Norton & Company.

United Nations Department of Public Information.
    1990   *The Blue Helmets: A Review of United Nations Peace-keeping*. New York: United Nations, Dept. of Public Information.

von Sponeck, Hans C.
    2006   *A Different Kind of War: The UN Sanctions Regime in Iraq*. New York: Berghahn Books.

Walker, Alice.
    1991   *Her Blue Body Everything We Know: Earthling Poems 1965-1990 Complete*. New York: Harcourt Brace Jovanovich Publishers.

Waller, Signe.
    2002   *Love and Revolution: A Political Memoir: People's History of the Greensboro Massacre, Its Setting and Aftermath*. Lanham, MD: Rowman & Littlefield.

Washington, James M., ed.
    1986   *A Testament of Hope: The Essential Writings and Speeches of Martin Luther King, Jr.* San Francisco: HarperSanFrancisco.

Waziyatawin.
    2008   *What Does Justice Look Like? The Struggle for Liberation in Dakota Homeland.* St. Paul: Living Justice Press.

Weaver, J. Denny.
    1987   *Becoming Anabaptist: The Origin and Significance of Sixteenth-Century Anabaptism.* Scottdale, PA: Herald Press.

Williams, George H.
    1999   *The Radical Reformation.* Third edition. Kirksville, MO: Sixteenth Century Journal Publications.

Wink, Walter.
    1992   *Engaging the Powers: Discernment and Resistance in a World of Domination.* Philadelphia: Fortress Press.

Wise, Tim J.
    2007   *White Like Me: Reflections on Race from a Privileged Son.* New York: Soft Skull Press.
    2005   *Affirmative Action: Racial Preference in Black and White.* New York: Routledge.

Worth, Richard.
    2006   *Dolores Huerta.* New York: Chelsea House.

Zehr, Howard.
    2002   *The Little Book of Restorative Justice.* Intercourse, PA: Good Books.
    1990   *Changing Lenses: A New Focus for Crime and Justice.* Scottdale, PA: Herald Press.

Zehr, Howard, and Barb Toews, eds.
    2004   *Critical Issues in Restorative Justice.* Portland: Criminal Justice Press and Willan Publishing.

Zur, Ofer.
    1991   "The Love of Hating: The Psychology of Enmity." *History of European Ideas* 13/4:345-69.

DUE